2013 中国财政发展报告
（英文版）
Report on China's Public Finance 2013
（English Version）

上海财经大学公共政策研究中心
Center for Public Policy Studies of SUFE

中国出版集团

世界图书出版公司

广州·上海·西安·北京

图书在版编目（CIP）数据

2013 中国财政发展报告：英文／上海财经大学公共政策研究中心编. —广州：世界图书出版广东有限公司，2014.6
　ISBN　978-7-5100-8178-1

　Ⅰ.①2…　Ⅱ.①上…　Ⅲ.①财政政策—研究报告—中国—2013—英文　Ⅳ.①F812.0

　中国版本图书馆 CIP 数据核字（2014）第 135084 号

2013 中国财政发展报告（英文版）

策划编辑　吴小丹
责任编辑　汪再祥
编辑邮箱　uyling@163.com
出版发行　世界图书出版广东有限公司
地　　址　广州市新港西路大江冲 25 号
http://www.gdst.com.cn
印　　刷　虎彩印艺股份有限公司
规　　格　787mm×1092mm　1/16
印　　张　10.25
字　　数　150 千字
版　　次　2014 年 6 月第 1 版　2014 年 10 月第 2 次印刷
ISBN　]978-7-5100-8178-1/F・0145
定　　价　42.00 元

《2013 中国财政发展报告》编委会

Editorial Committee of Report on China's Public Finance 2013

主　　　编：曾军平　刘小兵
副　主　编：朱为群　宋健敏　邓淑莲
编委会成员：邓淑莲　高　军　孔　晏
　　　　　　刘　伟　凌　云　刘小兵
　　　　　　宋健敏　阳　维　杨海燕
　　　　　　曾军平　朱为群

Chief Editor：Zeng Junping　Liu Xiaobing
Deputy Editor：Zhu Weiqun　Song Jianmin　Deng Shulian
Committee Members：Deng Shulian　Gao Jun　Kong Yan
　　　　　　　　　　Liu Wei　Ling Yun　Liu Xiaobing
　　　　　　　　　　Song Jianmin　Yang Wei　Yang Haiyan
　　　　　　　　　　Zeng Junping　Zhu Weiqun

Contents

1 Macroeconomic Performance

Affected by the Europe's sovereign-debt crisis, the global economy as well as many major economies continued to slow down in 2012. A forecast by the United Nations in October 2012 showed that the growth rate of entire economy of Europe might drop to -0.2%, and the growth rate of the Eurozone might fall to -0.5%, which is 2.0 percent lower than the previous year. Growths in emerging markets and developing countries were widely lower than that in 2011. Currently, though the United States posted a growth slightly higher than that in 2011, it was still impossible to set off the negative impacts on the global economy caused by the Eurozone recession.

In 2012, faced with increasingly complicated and severe international economic situation and arduous tasks of domestic reform, development and stability, China took the transformation of economic growth mode as the major task, strengthened and improved macro-control in time, and attached greater importance to the task of stabilizing growth. As a result, China maintained a good momentum of steady economic and social development. In a word, in 2012, the overall national economy maintained steady development, price increases dropped steadily, the position of agriculture as the foundation of the economy was further consolidated and the social situation remained stable.

Based on different economic activities, macroeconomy can be divided into production, distribution, consumption, accumulation and international trade. To this end, we shall analyze China's macroeconomic performance in 2012 in these five aspects, and make forecasts about its economic trend in 2013.

1.1 Performance of production activities in 2012

1.1.1 As its overall economy remained stable and its GDP slowed down in growth, China achieved a soft landing in its macroeconomy

As to the quarterly accumulative GDP growth, after the financial crisis of 2008, China's GDP reached its peak at 12.1% in the first quarter of 2010. After that, China's GDP slowed down all the way till 7.7% in the third quarter of 2012. As to the changes in the growth rate, the absolute value of GDP growth saw a big fall by 4.4 percentage points. However, as China accelerated adjustment of its economic structure and reform of its economic growth pattern and the global economic situation continued to slump, it is still a high growth that China's GDP growth rate remained at above 7.5%. Moreover, after the slow destocking process in the first three quarters, economic data of the fourth quarter released a clear signal that the economy will pick up slightly. Instead of falling, GDP growth rate was up by 0.1 percent over that of the same period of last year.

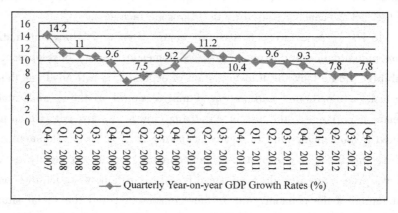

Figure 1.1 Quarterly Year-on-Year GDP Growth Rates in 2007-2012
Source: the National Bureau of Statistics of China.

1.1.2 While the secondary and tertiary industries slowed down in growth, added value of the primary industry grew up steadily

In 2012, China's grain output saw another harvest, marking the ninth consecutive year of growth. With policies on agriculture, farmers and rural areas steadily advanced, input in agricultural science further increased, and large-scale agricultural production widely promoted, China's agricultural production continued to increase. In 2012, the total output of summer grain was 129.95 million tons, increased 3.56 million tons over last year, with a growth rate of 2.8 percent. As a result of consecutive harvests, China's grain stock is plentiful, with the stock-consumption ratio up to 40%, well above the internationally recognized safety line of 17%-18%. This provides a crucial material base for China to maintain economic growth.

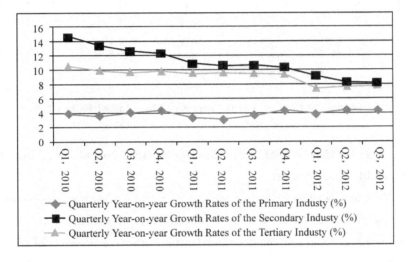

Figure 1.2 Quarterly Year-on-Year Growth Rates of Added Value of Three Industries

Source: National Bureau of Statistics of China.

1. 1. 3 Structural Proportions of Three Industries Remained the Basic Pattern of "Secondary, Tertiary and Primary" in 2012

Though the Chinese government has listed industrial restructuring as a work focus of the "12th five-year" plan, it is impossible to achieve it overnight. Time is needed to go through progressive adjustments and get used to them. Especially when economic and political situations tend to become increasingly complicated at home and abroad, China's economic restructuring shall be confronted with greater difficulties and challenges.

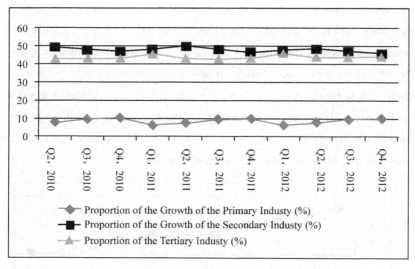

Figure 1. 3 Changes to Proportions of Three Industries in GDP

Source: National Bureau of Statistics of China.

1. 1. 4 China's PMI kept falling in the first half of 2012, but went up steadily since August

As one of leading indicators adopted world-wide to monitor macroeconomic tendencies, purchasing managers index (PMI) is calculated and derived from monthly surveys of company purchasing managers, involves all business processes from purchasing to production and circulation, and has powerful functions in giving forecasts and warnings. PMI usually takes 50% as the critical point between a strong economy and a weak one. A PMI reading above 50% suggests economic expansion while one below 50% indicates contraction. Based on China's PMI results in 2012, non-manufacturing PMIs were generally higher than manufacturing ones, indicating that economic expansion of the non-manufacturing sector continued to be greater than the manufacturing sector as that in 2011. In the first eight months of 2012, PMI indexes for the manufacturing sector kept dropping, reaching the bottom at 49. 2 in August. After that, it started to rebound and hit 50. 6 in November. This indicated that China's macroeconomic control policy began to have effects on real economy and the trend of economic recovery was quite evident.

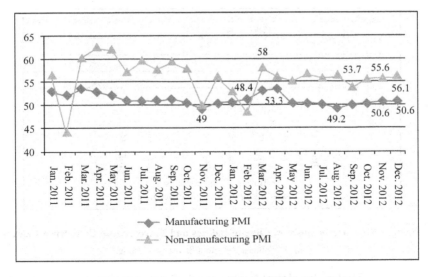

Figure 1.4 Manufacturing and Non-manufacturing PMIs

Source: National Bureau of Statistics of China.

1.1.5 Though China's business climate index and entrepreneur confidence index continued to drop, they remained above 100, which showed that the macroeconomic climate tended to stabilize and was on the rise

Business climate index (BCI) reflects entrepreneurs' expectations for macroeconomic outlook, business production, operation and future development. The index ranges from zero to 200 points, with 100 as the threshold. A reading of more than 100 indicates a rising or improved climate, a reading below 100 shows a sign of a declining or downturn environment, while a reading equal to 100 means no significant change to the economic climate. Based on changes to BCIs in 2012, BCIs maintained at above 100, but their values fell from Quarter 1 to Quarter 3, indicating that though entrepreneurs were confident in the future economic growth, their confidence reduced slightly. Entering the fourth quarter, as negative factors faded away one by one, both indicators climbed up to 124.4 and 120.4 respectively.

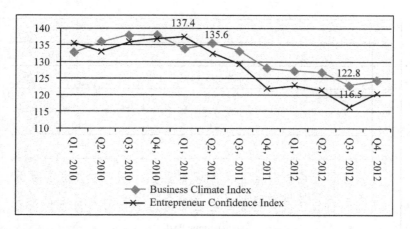

Figure 1.5 Quarterly Business Climate Indexes and Entrepreneur Confidence Indexes

Source: National Bureau of Statistics of China.

1.1.6 Under the global background of quantitative easing, China's prices declined steadily

After hitting the peak of 6.5% in July 2011, China's CPI continued to decline and maintained at a level of about 2% in the second half of 2012. CPI remained low because of impacts of various factors, especially the real estate control policies stably implemented and food prices progressively reduced. Notably, however, China's PPI continued to drop, even posted negative growths for many months in a row. China has participated in depth in the international labor-division system for many years, and its industrial production features "massive imports and exports". Nevertheless, China's exports were largely affected by the world's lasting economic downturn. For example, just in the first half of 2012, the growth rate of China's exports was nearly 2/3 less than that in the same period of last year. As a result, overcapacity became a matter of fact in the area of production. When export became difficult, entrepreneurs chose to reduce investment on raw material and equipment rather than expand their workshops and increase work forces. This shift constituted the most fundamental reason for PPI to turn downward. It reflects from a different perspective that China's manufacturing sector was currently under tremendous growth pressures. Some experts even analyzed GDP deflator and PPI changes to conclude that China's real economy may have been stuck in deflation.

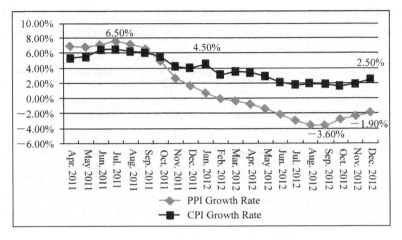

Figure 1.6 Changes to CPIs and PPIs

Source: National Bureau of Statistics of China.

1.1.7 As industrial production slowed down in growth, the heavy industry dropped at a pace greater than the light industry which caused their growth rates to become approximate

Among China's industrial growths over the years, the heavy industry has been growing faster than the light industry in most cases, thus steadily uplifting the proportion of the heavy industry in China's industrial production. In 2012, it had some changes and growth rates of the light industry were higher than that of the heavy industry in some months. The light industry refers to 45 industries of 19 sectors that mainly provide consumer products and produce hand tools, such as food, paper-making and home appliances, covering clothing, food, housing, transportation, and industrial portfolios in the area of consumption and presenting significant features of "meeting domestic needs, being exported abroad, supporting employment, and providing services for agriculture, farmers and rural areas". The heavy industry means the industrial system that, based on the industry of energy and raw material, is mainly composed of industries manufacturing top-grade durable consumer goods, equipment, electronic and electrical appliances, and chemicals, including metallurgy, machinery, energy, chemical and building material, functioning as a fundamental industry providing technological equipment, power and raw material for various sectors of the national economy. It provides the material basis for realization and expansion of social reproduction. Growth rates of light and heavy industries in 2012 were reflections of changes to macroeconomic situations at home and abroad.

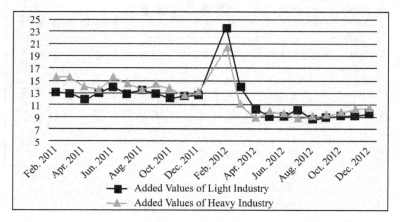

Figures 1.7 Growth Rates of Light and Heavy Industries
Data Source: National Bureau of Statistics of China.

1.1.8 Based on cumulative growth rates of industrial added value by regions, western, central and eastern China slowed down in growth, and were in an ascending order when sorted by their growth rates

According to cumulative growth rates in the first 11 months, western China had an average growth of 14.9%, central China 13.8% and eastern China only 10.55%. Among the top 10 regions, 5 were located in western China, 2 in central China and 3 in eastern China; and of the last 10 cities, 1 was from western China, 2 from central China and 7 from eastern China. Moreover, around the country, Shanghai achieved a growth of only 2.7%, largely lower than the national level. This, on one hand, was attributed to different growth base of these regions. Developed areas had bigger growth base than central and western China. On the other, it was caused by differences in the industrial structure of these regions. For example, as China promoted structural adjustment, Shanghai has been active in adjusting its industrial structure and enhancing efforts in developing the third industry, especially financial services, thus having powerful impacts on growths of industrial added value. However, this also explains from a different perspective that China's industrial growth has been shifting toward central and western areas.

Table 1.1 Cumulative growth rates of industrial added value in 2012

(by regions)

Ranking	Province	Cumulative growth rates	Ranking	Province	Cumulative growth rates
1	Shannxi	16.6	17	Gansu	14.6
2	Chongqing	16.3	18	Jilin	14.1
3	Anhui	16.2	19	Ningxia	13.8
4	Guizhou	16.2	20	Hebei	13.4
5	Tianjin	16.1	21	Xinjiang	12.7
6	Sichuan	16.1	22	Jiangsu	12.6
7	Guangxi	15.9	23	Shanxi	11.9
8	Yunnan	15.6	24	Shandong	11.4
9	Fujian	15.2	25	Heilongjiang	10.5
10	Tibet	15.1	26	Liaoning	9.9
11	Inner Mongolia	14.8	27	Hainan	8.9
12	Qinghai	14.8	28	Guangdong	8.4
13	Jiangxi	14.7	29	Zhejiang	7.1
14	Henan	14.6	30	Beijing	7
15	Hubei	14.6	31	Shanghai	2.9
16	Hunan	14.6			

Data Source: National Bureau of Statistics of China.

1.1.9 Urban registered unemployment rate remained at 4.1% for eight consecutive quarters since September 2010

At the end of year 2012, the number of employed people in China was 767.04 million, and that in urban areas was 371.02 million. The newly increased employed people in urban areas numbered 12.66 million. The urban unemployment rate through unemployment registration was 4.1 percent at the year end, maintaining the same level as 2011 and was unchanged for 8 consecutive quarters since September 2010. A statistical analysis conducted by China Human Resource Market Information Monitoring Center in Quarter 3 of 2012 based on information of market supplies and demands provided by public employment institutions in 100 cities around the country came to the following major conclusions: (1) In general, labor supplies and demands in the market were well balanced; market supplies and demands increased when compared with the same period of last year, but reduced when compared with the previous quarter. (2) Compared with the previous year, while market demands in eastern areas slightly reduced, supplies and demands largely increased in central and western areas. Compared with last quarter, market supplies and demands reduced in all these areas. (3) More than 80% of labor demands were centered around such industries as manufacturing, services to households and other services, wholesale and retail trade, lodging and catering services, leasing and business services, construction; compared with the same period of last year, demands for labor forces by industries including construction, services to households and other services witnessed great increases, while those by industries including manufacturing, wholesale and retail trade, lodging and catering services had slight growths. (4) Beyond 90% of demands were from enterprises; domestic enterprises, enterprises funded by compatriots from Hong Kong, Macao and Taiwan, foreign-funded enterprises saw growths over the previous year. (5) Market demands for medium and senior skilled talents exceeded market supplies; compared with the same period of last year, demands for medium and senior skilled workforces increased substantially.

1.2. Distribution in 2012

1.2.1 Though income of urban and rural residents grew faster than GDP, there continued to be a big discrepancy between them

Income of urban and rural residents gradually rose up at paces greater than GDP growth. Although cash income of rural residents surpassed per-capita disposable income of urban residents in terms of growth rates, there remained a huge income gap between rural residents and urban residents. Income distribution shall continue to be a top priority of China's economic reform at present and for a period in the future. It is also a crucial factor in China's overall economic development and social stability. Affected and restricted by a number of factors, China has been slow to launch a plan for its income distribution reform, which partly reflected that income distribution reform is facing with tremendous difficulties and pressures. Nevertheless, we must see that the current problem of income distribution gap is not only an economic problem, but also a political one that matters the social stability and long-term security of the country. As an important regulator of income secondary distribution, the government should adopt more policies and measures to narrow the income gap, especially that between rural and urban residents.

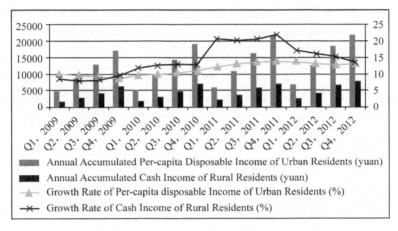

Figure 1.8 Income of Urban and Rural Residents in 2009-2012
Source: the database of Wind Info.

1.2.2 Income structure of rural residents had no significant change

According to income defined in the national economic accounting system, income earned from various sources by rural residents is classified into four categories, namely, income from wages and salaries, income from household operations, income from properties and income from transfers. In 2012, while total income of rural residents increased on a year-by-year basis, its structure had no significant change. For rural residents, income from such operation as sales of agricultural products is the most important source, and income from wages and salaries also accounts for a great proportion, but that from properties stood for quite a small proportion. Combined with the current problem and situation of income distribution in China, raising income of rural residents should be an important part of China's reform on income distribution system. In terms of income from properties, due to their disadvantages in capital, knowledge and technology, rural resident lack the ability to obtain income from transferring these production factors. Therefore, it will be very difficult to increase this part of income. The government and the society, however, can take some actions in terms of transfer payment as an important means to regulate secondary distribution.

Table 1.2 Per-capita Income of Rural Residents and Its Structure

Year	Income from wages and salaries		Income from household operations		Income from properties		Income from transfers		Total Income
	Sub-total	Percentage	Sub-total	Percentage	Sub-total	Percentage	Sub-total	Percentage	Total
Dec. 2009	2058	32.82%	3591	57.27%	148	2.37%	473	7.55%	6270
Dec. 2010	2428	34.25%	3955	55.80%	168	2.37%	537	7.58%	7089
Dec. 2011	2960	34.26%	4810	55.69%	186	2.15%	683	7.90%	8639
Dec. 2012	3442	35.29%	5277	54.10%	202	2.08%	832	8.53%	9754

Data Source: National Bureau of Statistics of China.

1.2.3 China's monthly fiscal revenue saw a dramatic decline

Data reveals that China's year-on-year growth rate of fiscal revenue stood at 24.8% in December 2011, but declined to about 12% in 2012. It should be admitted that this was a huge drop, which was mainly caused by the declined growth rate of macroeconomy. Meanwhile, the reform of national tax system and other factors also produced great impacts on it. Even so, the monthly cumulative year-on-year growth rate of fiscal revenue was still higher

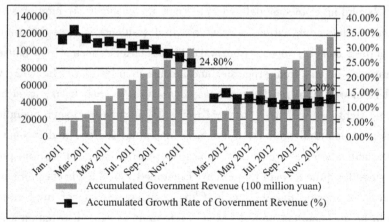

Figure 1.9 Monthly National Fiscal Revenue in 2011-2012

Data Source: the website of the Ministry of Finance of the People's Republic of China.

than that of GDP in the same period. It should be noted that this growth rate was lower than that of income of urban and rural residents.

1.2.4 Proportion of quarterly national fiscal revenue in GDP went up steadily

Though China's national fiscal revenue is collected from diversified sources, taxation remains the major source. Based on data currently available, it is obvious that shares and impacts of the government in income distribution has been further intensified, which in turn requires the government to take more responsibilities and play bigger role in income redistribution.

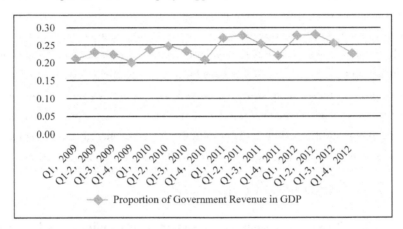

Figure 1.10 Proportions of Quarterly National Revenue in GDP

Notes: Quarterly cumulative fiscal revenue refers to monthly cumulative fiscal revenue in March, June, September and December.

Data Source: National Bureau of Statistics of China and the Ministry of Finance.

1.2.5 Revenue and profits made by industrial enterprises above the designated size went down from the previous year, especially that the profits dropped drastically

China remains an industry-dominated country. The profits made by the industrial enterprises above the designated size in 2012 were 5,557.8 billion yuan, an increase of 5.3 percent over the same period of last year. Profits made in December 2012 totaled 895.2 billion yuan, up 17.3% over the corresponding period of last year. It should be admitted that there was indeed a sign of improvement at the end of 2012.

Within 41 branches of industrial divisions, the profits of 29 industrial divisions increased year-on-year, that of 11 declined, and 1 turned to get net profits from loss, year-on-year. Of which, the profits of production and supply of electric power and heat power expanded by 69.1%, and that of agro-food processing industry rose by 20.6%, both having leading performance; that of ferrous metal mining and processing significantly decreased by 37.3%, and that of processing of petroleum, coking, processing of nuclear fuel turned to get net profits from loss, year-on-year.

Data in the above show that there are currently tremendous difficulties and pressures over China's real economy. Constrained by a series of factors, including the transformation of economic structure, macroeconomic slowdown and global economic downturn, development and growth of China's secondary industry had an obvious trend of slowdown. Due to the nature of capital that seeks profits, these areas were confronted with enormous market and capital pressures. If macroeconomic fundamentals have not any significant improvement, these problems shall be transmitted to other economic areas. Thus, difficulties faced by the real economy are worth attention from all parties.

1.3 Consumption in 2012

1.3.1 Total retail sales of consumer goods maintained high-speed growth, but slowed down in recent years

Since the 16th CPC national congress, with the continuous and rapid economic growth, consumer goods supplied in the market increased in kinds and quantities, and their qualities were apparently improved, thus to greatly satisfy multi-level and diversified consumption demands of the residents. Efficient market supply kept rising, resulting in the establishment of a market pattern dominated by the buyers. Consumers have more freedom and space for selection in shopping and consumption. Especially, substantial increases of IT products represented by mobile phones and computers, automobiles making transportation more convenient, house decorating products manufactured to improve people's living conditions and life quality, and home appliances made the structure of market supply and demand more reasonable to continuously expand the room for residents to select consumer goods.

As income of urban and rural residents jacked up, their consumption power were intensified and the market size of consumer goods kept growing and maintained a trend of steady and rapid growth in general. Total retail sales of consumer goods increased from 4.8 trillion yuan in 2002 to 18.4 trillion yuan in 2011, rising up by 2.8 times, thus an annual growth of 16.1%. The market of consumer goods has entered a period of rapid growth. By 2012, total retail sales of consumer goods in the first 11 months amounted to 18.68 trillion yuan. Compared with last month, the index of total retail sales of consumer goods has remained above 100 since 2004 and hit the peak at 121.6 in 2008. As of 2012, total retail sales in the first 11 months had exceeded that achieved throughout 2011. However, while the size went up, we found that the index gradually declined since 2010, indicating that the growth of total retail sales of consumer goods were slowing down.

It should be pointed out that though total retail sales of consumer goods represents the general situation of social consumption, its notion is not the same of consumption in economics. In statistics, the index also deems some purchases by residents for purpose of investment as consumption. Nevertheless, it does not prevent us from using the index as a main parameter to analyze the general trend of social consumption.

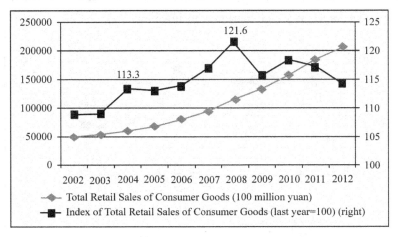

Figure 1.11 Total Retail Sales of Consumer Goods and Its Indexes

Data source: the database of Wind Info.

1.3.2 Total retail sales of consumer goods gradually reduced in the first half of 2012 and picked up step by step in the second half, with its growth in rural areas faster than that in cities

Based on monthly data in 2011 and 2012 (due to data availability, data of January and February 2012 were missing), as affected by the Spring Festival, total retail sales of consumer goods reached the peak at 18.2% in December 2011. After entering 2012, the index declined continuously in the first half of the year, reached the bottom at 13.1% in July and went up gradually thereafter. Viewed from the perspective of structure, the changing curve of total retail sales of consumer goods of the whole society was highly in line with that of urban areas, both lines almost coinciding. But data of rural areas had greater deviations. In 2011, total retail sales of consumer goods in rural areas were much lower than that of the whole society and urban areas. In 2012, however, it was largely above the latter. This shift indicates that steadily accelerated growth of farmers' income and gradually expanded update of consumption structure have released consumption potentials in rural areas, thus proactively promoting steady development of the entire market of consumer goods and presenting a picture where markets in urban and rural areas realized growth and flourishing at the same time. However, urban areas continued to be major forces of social consumption in China.

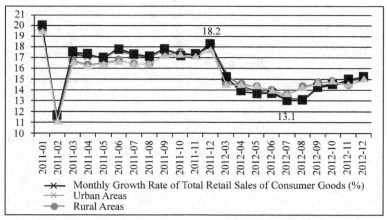

Figure 1.12 Monthly Growths of Total Retail Sales of Consumer Goods in Urban and Rural Areas

Data Source: the database of Wind Info.

1.3.3 Rapid growth of online consumption

In recent years, with the rapid spread of the Internet, informationization level of Chinese households has been largely promoted. Thanks to its various advantages, such as abundant supplies, affordable prices, convenient shopping and door-to-door delivery, online consumption has developed into a popular mode of consumption among Chinese residents. Especially, new regulations on third-party payment platforms set up by the government and non-card payment platforms launched by the Unionpay provided online consumption and other new type consumption modes with more conveniences and better circumstances, thus triggering the residents to rush into shopping via the Internet. Statistical data reveals that retail sales of mail marketing and electronic sales in 2011 were nearly twice that of 2010. At the same time, new technologies and products kept emerging and helped promote consumption of relative products. In 2011, total retail sales of communication equipment by enterprises (organizations) above limited amounts grew up by 27.5%, a growth rate of 5.7 percentage points higher than that of 2010, which was the highest growth rate among 16 kinds of goods. As online shopping and payment become a mode favored by numerous residents, online consumption presented a momentum of rapid growth, emerging as a new focus of consumption.

According to data disclosed by China E-commerce Research Center (100ec. cn), China's online shopping transactions in the first quarter of 2012 totaled 233.6 billion yuan, a year-on-year growth of 42.8% over the first quarter of 2011. It reached 511.9 billion yuan by the end of June 2012, a year-on-year growth of 46.6%, and 1.3205 trillion yuan by the end of December 2012, up 64.7%.

Data shows that as of December 2012, Tmall remained No. 1 in China's B2C (business to customer) market, accounting for 52.1% of the market size; Jingdong Mall was at the second place, accounting for 22.3%; Suning E-go, at the third place, stood for 3.6%; and other e-commerce companies at the fourth to tenth places were respectively: Tencent, Amazon, Vancl, Coo8 (Gome), Dangdang, Yixun and Newegg.

In terms of C2C (customer to customer) market, data reveals that by the end of December 2012, Taobao continued to "monopolize" the market. As of June 2012, Taobao accounted for 96.4% of the total, while Paipai stood for 3.4% and Eachnet 0.2%.

Figure 1. 13 Transactions in China's Online Shopping Market

Data Source: China E-commerce Research Center, www. 100ec. cn.

1.3.4 Government expenditures grew up steadily

Public revenue and expenditures maintained growth in 2012. According to Figures for Fiscal Revenue and Expenditures in 2012 released by the Ministry of Finance, national expenditure exceeded the budgeted figure of 12. 4300 trillion yuan and amounted to 12. 5712 trillion yuan, an increase of 1. 6464 trillion yuan over last year or 15. 1% ; and national revenue reached 11. 7210 trillion yuan, an increase of 1. 3335 trillion yuan or 12. 8% over 2011.

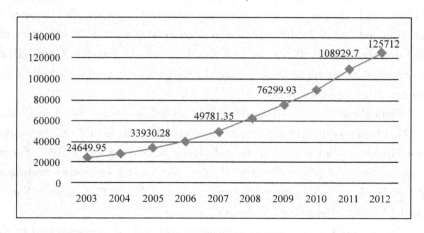

Figure 1. 14 China's Fiscal Expenditures in 2003-2012 (Unit: 100 Million Yuan)

Data Source: the website of the Ministry of Finance.

1.3.5 Government spending structure shifted from a public finance "focusing on economic growth" to one "focusing on people's livelihood"

As China adhered to focusing on economic construction since its reform and opening-up, fiscal expenditures of the Chinese government tended to focus on economic construction and government administration, instead of on government consumption that provides public services and goods. Therefore, China's public finance had kept "focusing on economic growth" rather than "focusing on people's livelihood" for years. Due to long-term "economic-focused public finance", China's inputs in public goods and services were insufficient, especially low spending on education, culture, health care, and social security, causing it difficult for people to go to school, find a job, go to hospital, live a happy life after retirement and buy a house. Chinese households have to save a large part of their limited income so as to spend on things that should be borne by the government. As a result, China's savings tend to be highly precautionary, which heavily held back residents' spending power and level. Therefore, it was not household consumption itself but functions of the Chinese government not thoroughly transformed that continued to reduce contributions of consumption to GDP. During the 12th five-year plan period, fiscal policies give top priority to people's livelihood. Constantly increased spending on consumption not only had direct impacts on pulling up final consumption ratio, but also largely released households' spending power. Its indirect effects on promoting the final consumption ratio cannot be neglected.

In 2012, the Chinese government continued to increase spending on people's livelihood, and set up major targets for spending related to people's livelihood through detailed and specific expenditure items. In *Report on the Implementation of Central and Local Budgets for* 2011 *and on Draft Central and Local Budgets for* 2012, budgetary spending on people's livelihood, including education, medical and health care, social security and employment, housing and culture amount to 36.91% of total expenditure targets, including 378.132 billion yuan appropriated for education in the central government budgets, up 16.4%. According to preliminary estimates, China's government spending on education will reach about 2198.4 billion yuan. Calculated on the basis of GDP expectations, government spending on education shall account for above 4% of China's GDP in 2012. Social security and employment is another focus of China's fiscal expenditures, accounting for above 10% of total expenditures in its budget. Based on figures achieved, all expenditure items on people's livelihood have reached their targets. Education spending reached 2. 1165 trillion yuan, a growth of 466. 7 billion yuan over last year, or up 28. 3%; spending on medical and health care totaled 719. 9 billion yuan, an increase of 76. 9 billion yuan, or up 12%; that on social security and employment amounted to 1. 2542 trillion yuan, a rise of 143. 2 billion yuan, up 12. 9%; the appropriation for guaranteeing adequate housing was 444. 6 billion yuan, a gain of 62. 5 billion yuan, up 16. 4%.

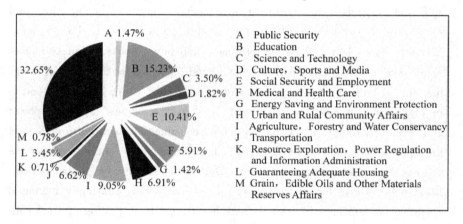

Figure 1. 15 Proportions of Major Expenditure Items in National Fiscal Budget in 2012

Data Source: Based on *Report on the Implementation of Central and Local Budgets for* 2011 *and on Draft Central and Local Budgets for* 2012, http://www. gov. cn/2012lh/content_2093446. htm

1. 4 Economic Accumulations in 2012

From the perspective of accounting, national economic accumulations include accumulation of fix assets, accumulation of financial assets, accumulation brought about by price changes and that by other non-economic activities. Due to China's current accounting level and data, we can only find data about fixed assets and financial assets. So we will mainly illustrate transactions of fixed assets and financial assets in this section.

1.4.1 Total investment on fixed assets gradually increased at a slower rate in 2012

Data reveals that monthly investment on fixed data in 2012 was basically higher than that in the same period of 2011, so the aggregate should be higher than that of 2011. In terms of growth rate, the cumulative year-on-year growth rate of investment on fixed assets in 2012 reduced sharply from 23.8% in November 2011 to 20.6% in December 2012. This change was in line with the overall decline of China's GDP growth and government policies and measures adopted to transform China's economic growth mode.

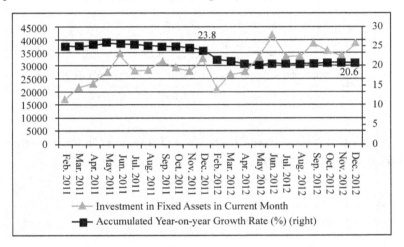

Figure 1.16 Monthly Investment on Fixed Assets and Year-on-year Growth Rates of Accumulated Investment in 2011-2012

Data Source: the database of Wind Info.

1.4.2 Overall investment in fixed assets of the three industries witnessed rapid growth

Judged by the growth of investment in fixed assets of different industries, that of the primary industry posted a growth, while that of the secondary industry and that of the tertiary industry were on the decline. However, among the overall industrial investment, the primary industry continued to account for a low proportion at around 2.47%; the tertiary industry had the largest proportion coming to 54.04%. This, on one hand, reflects that the Chinese government has increased efforts in supporting agriculture, farmers and rural areas, and on the other, indicates that based on the overall national economy, the secondary and tertiary industries have absolute advantages in investment-driven growth.

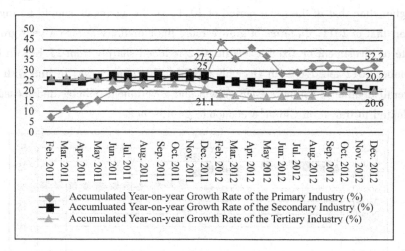

Figure 1. 17 Year-on-year Growth Rates of Investment in Fixed Assets of the Three Industries in 2011-2012

Source: the database of Wind Info.

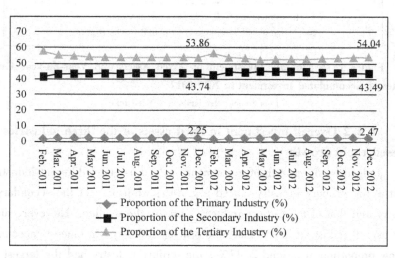

Figure 1. 18 Proportions of Investment in the Three Industries in 2011-2012

Source: the database of Wind Info.

1. 4. 3 Investment in fixed assets saw dramatic slides in the first three quarters of 2012

In terms of structure, western areas, local projects and joint ventures with Hong Kong or Macau reduced largely and investment in real estate development had the largest drop. Analyzed by regions, investment growth in western areas decreased largely by 5. 8 percentages points, while that in central and eastern areas declined by around 4 percentage points. Based on project ownership, central government projects were the only kind of investment that registered growth in the table below. From the perspective of enterprise type, joint ventures with Hong Kong or Macau had the largest reduction of 11. 9 percentage points, far beyond that of domestic- and foreign-funded ones. In particular, affected by the real estate control policy, investment in real estate development had the largest reduction of 11. 7 percentage points in 2012.

2012 was the second year for China to carry out its "twelfth five-year" plan. Historically speaking, many new projects are launched in the first year of each "five-year plan" period, and project investment will come to its peak in the second year after the launch. Normally, growth rate in the second year is more rapid than the first year. The drop of investment in fixed assets in 2012 was, on one hand, affected by changes in domestic and international macroeconomic situations, and on the other, resulted from China's active adjustment of the growth mode. In addition, strict real estate control policies, capital chain rupture incurred by folk financing and impacts of private entrepreneurs absconding were important causes for the slide of investment growth in 2012.

Table 1. 3 Growths of Investment on Fixed Assets in 2011 First Three Quarters of and 2012   (Excluding Rural Households): %

	Year 2011	Year 2012	Change
Investment by regions			
Eastern area	21. 3	17. 8	− 3. 5
Central area	28. 8	25. 8	− 3. 0
Western area	29. 2	24. 2	− 5. 0
Projects owned by			
Central government	− 9. 7%	5. 9	15. 6
Local government	27. 2%	21. 7	− 5. 5

(**Continued**)

	Year 2011	Year 2012	Change
Enterprise types			
Domestic enterprise	24.7	21.2	-3.5
Joint venture with funds from Hong Kong and Macao	19.9	8.0	-11.9
Foreign-funded	12	14.5	2.5
Investment in real estate development	27.9	16.2	-11.7
Private investment	34.3	24.8	-9.5

Source: Economic Blue Book 2013, compiled by Chen Jiagui and Li Yang, Social Sciences Academic Press, December 2012.

National Bureau of Statistics of China, Private Investment in Fixed Assets for January to December 2012, Private Investment in Fixed Assets for January to December 2011.

1.4.4 The overall size of the stock market increased, but its growth structure was unbalanced

Data in the table reveals that compared with 2011, market sizes of all securities saw increases in 2012. Among them, stock index futures posted the highest growth rate of 104.97%, while stocks had the lowest growth rate of 0.72%. This was closely related to performance of China's stock market in 2012. It can be known from the diagram that stock indexes at Shanghai and Shenzhen stock exchanges kept moving downward, even with the Shanghai A-share composite index falling below 2000 points. While market prices were poor in performance, trading volume declined simultaneously. In 2012, the average market earnings multiples remained at a low level. As of October 30, 2012, the average earnings multiples in Shanghai and Shenzhen stock markets were respectively 11.17 and 20.93, which highlighted the market investment value. However, as investors worried about the downward risks of the national economy and the external downturn in the international economic environment, market activity remained at a low level. For the stock market that had been declining for 6 years in a row, the investors were still in a strong wait-and-see mood.

Table 1.4 Structure of China's Stock Market

Financial tools	December 14, 2012		December 31, 2011		Data in 2012 over that in 2011	
	Market size (100 million)	Percentage (%)	Market size (100 million)	Percentage (%)	Change in Size (%)	Change in percentage (%)
Stock index futures	702.69	0.14	342.83	0.08	104.97	0.06
Closed-end funds	1778.33	0.36	1116.09	0.25	59.34	0.11
Commodity futures	7020.50	1.42	4534.94	1.00	54.81	0.42
open-end fund	24765.69	5.00	20447.43	4.50	21.12	0.5
Stock	216335.48	43.67	214785.49	47.28	0.72	−3.61
Bonds	244767.67	49.41	213101.81	46.90	14.86	2.51
Total	495370.36	100.00	454328.59	100.00	9.03	0

Source: the database of Wind Info.

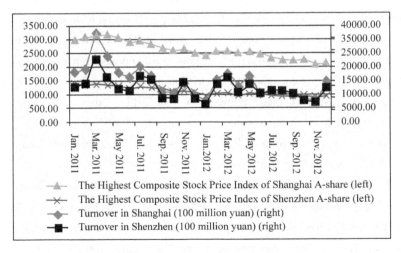

Figure 1.19 Monthly A-share Price Indexes and Turnovers in Shanghai and Shenzhen Stock Exchanges in 2011-2012

Data Source: the database of Wind Info.

1. 4. 5 The central bank adopted a variety of means to increase money supply and steadily pushed forward the process of RMB interest rate marketization

In 2012, the People's Bank of China took a package of methods to implement a prudent but a little expansionary monetary policy to increase money supply in order to support the economic growth on the decline. As prices remained low, the major objective of the monetary policy was directed from preventing inflation to maintaining growth. In terms of market operation, based on the changes in liquidity supply, reverse repo operations were conducted to meet the reasonable demands of the banking system for liquidity and to guide market interest rates to move in a stable manner. Meanwhile, measures were taken to guide financial institutions to optimize the credit structure. The reform of financial institutions continued to make progress, and the flexibility of the RMB exchange-rate regime increased. Under the combined effects of a number of policy measures, such as open market operations, the deposit reserve requirement ratio, central bank lending and re-discounting, interest rates, and counter-cyclical macro-prudential measures, growth in the supply of aggregate money accelerated notably, which effectively maintained the stability of the financial system and the stable performance of macroeconomic.

At end-2012, broad money (M2) stood at 97. 42 trillion yuan, increasing by 13. 8% year-on-year, up 0. 2 percentage points from end-2011. Narrow money (M1) registered 30. 87 trillion yuan, rising by 6. 5% year-on-year, down 1. 4 percentage points from end-2011. Currency in circulation (M0) posted 5. 47 trillion yuan, increasing by 7. 7% year-on-year, down 6. 1 percentage points from end-2011. In terms of other financial indexes: At end-2012, outstanding RMB loans amounted to 62. 99 trillion yuan, while RMB deposits registered an outstanding balance of 91. 74 trillion yuan. RMB loans registered an increase of 8. 20 trillion yuan for the full year, up 732 billion yuan year-on-year. RMB deposits rose by 10. 81 trillion yuan for the full year, up 1. 17 trillion yuan year-on-year. The lending interest rates of financial institutions declined further. In September, the weighted average lending rate offered to non-financial enterprises and other sectors posted 6. 97% , a reduction of 0. 09 percentage points from June. At end-September, the central parity of the RMB against the US dollar was 6. 3410 yuan per dollar, a depreciation of 0. 25% from end-June, whereas the real effective exchange rate of the RMB depreciated 0. 99%.

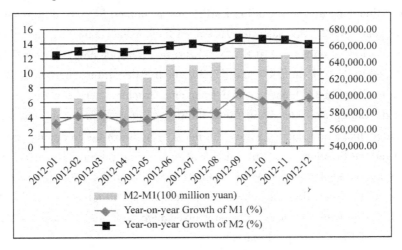

Figure 1. 20 Changes to Money Supply in 2012

Data Source: the website of the People's Bank of China.

1.4.6 Total social financing steadily increased, with the financing structure further optimized

As China makes further efforts to diversify financing modes and to innovate financial tools, new loans of financial institutions are not enough to describe the relationship between China's finance and real economy. Central economic working conferences held in December 2010 and December 2011, and Government Work Report delivered in March 2011 and March 2012 proposed to "maintain reasonable growth in total social financing". The People's Bank of China started to officially release data of total social financing in 2011. After operations in more than one year, total social financing has become an important index for China's macroeconomic regulation and control in 2012. According to *Monthly Data of Total Social Financing since* 2002 and *Annual Data and Structure of Total Social Financing since* 2002 released by the People's Bank of China on September 13, 2012, China's social financing increased from 2 trillion in 2002 to 12. 83 trillion in 2011, an average annual growth of 22. 9%, 6. 1 percentage points higher than RMB loans of the same period. The ratio of total social financing to GDP in 2011 was 27. 1%, up 10. 4 percentage points from 2002.

Analyzed by the structure, RMB loans declined in proportions: In 2002, other financing modes excluding RMB loans accounted for a small percentage. That year, RMB loans stood for 91. 9% of total social financing, and other financing modes only stood at 8. 1%. However, the percentage of RMB loans reduced to 73. 8% in 2006 and 57. 3% in the first three quarters of 2012. This explains that China's social financing structure has been further optimized. Enterprises can obtain funds through diversified financing modes, including stocks and bonds, which can not only optimize the financing structure and reduce financing cost, but also lead in multiple powers to oversee enterprise operation and promote the healthy operation of the enterprises. At the same time, diversified financing modes shall boost the size of China's stock market to provide investors with more investment tools and deepen the development of China's capital market.

1.5 China's International Trade in 2012

1.5.1 Monthly cumulative growth rates of imports and exports saw a sharp decline, but total trade surplus maintained a momentum of growth

On December 5, 2012, Pascal Lamy, director-general of the World Trade Organization, delivered to WTO member countries the annual report *"Overview of Developments in the International Trading Environment"*. The report shows that world trade growth in 2012 fell to only 2. 5%, down 50% from the previous year; export growth of developed countries was only 1. 5% while that of developing countries stood at 3. 5%. The report forecasts that the volume of trade growth in 2013 shall be at 4. 5%, still below the long-term annual average of 5. 4% for the last 20 years.

Facing the severe world trade situation, growth rates of China's imports and exports registered dramatic declines in 2012. Monthly year-on-year growth rates of imports dropped sharply from above 25% in 2011 to around 5% in 2012. Compared with the global growth rate, we think this was not easy.

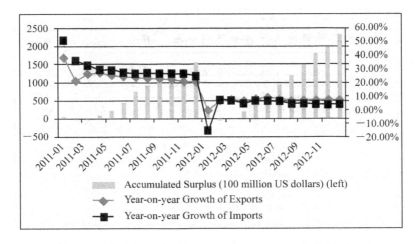

Figure 1.21 China's Imports and Exports in 2011-2012

Data Source: the database of Wind Info.

1.5.2 Proportions of imports and exports by state-owned enterprises reduced, that by foreign-funded enterprises remained stable, and that by other enterprises went up significantly

It can be seen from the diagram that proportions of imports and exports by foreign-funded enterprises stood at about 50% respectively, accounting for half of China's foreign trade. Proportions of imports and exports by state-owned enterprises declined in 2012: they were 27.3% and 12.8% respectively in December 2011, but both reduced to 25.97% and 11.25% respectively in December 2012. In contrast, contributions to imports and exports by other enterprises saw huge growths in the same year: proportion of exports by other enterprises rose up from 32.95% in December 2011 to 41.45% in December 2012; corresponding proportion of imports grew up from 23.70% in December 2011 to about 28.91%. This explains that among China's foreign trade in 2012, contributions made by private enterprises increased dramatically. This mainly attributed to measures adopted by the Chinese government after the outbreak of the financial crisis, which triggered private enterprises to actively improve their capability in fierce market competition and significantly enhance their sense of innovation.

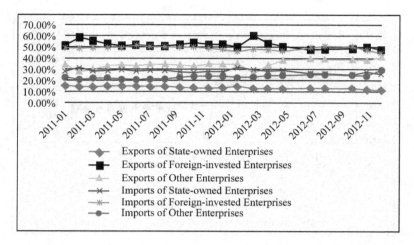

Figure 1. 22 Percentages of Monthly Imports and Exports by Enterprises of Different Ownership in 2011-2012

Data Source: Statistics of China Customs.

1. 5. 3 Analyzed by countries (and regions), trade between China and emerging markets saw rapid growth in 2012①

In terms of exports: in 2012, the United States remained the largest destination of China's exports. China's exports to America amounted to 351.8 billion dollars, up 8.4% year on year; Exports to EU, ASEAN and Japan that followed stood at 333.99 billion dollars, 151.65 billion dollars and 151.64 billion dollars, respectively a growth of −6.2%, 20.7% and 2.3% year on year. The drop in exports to EU was related to the European debt crisis that was not solved for a long time. Reduced demands in EU and the rise of trade protectionism were major causes for the drop in exports to EU. At the same time, China's trade with emerging markets saw rapid growth. Among the BRICs, China's exports to Russia had the largest growth of 13.2%; China's exports to ASEAN achieved a growth rate of 20.2%, largely above the overall export growth rate of 7%, which further strengthened ASEAN's position as the third largest trade partner of China.

In terms of imports: in 2012, China's imports from EU, the United

---

① Chen Jiagui and Li Yang, Analysis and Forecasts of China's Economic Situation in 2013, Social Sciences Academic Press, December 2012

States, Japan and ASEAN grew up by 0.4%, 8.8%, -8.6% and 1.5% respectively. Japan's exports to China reduced sharply mainly due to domestic boycott of Japan-made products, especially auto products, as a result of the Diaoyu Islands dispute. In contrast, China's cumulative imports from the BRIC countries in the first eight months of 2012 reached 110.22 billion US dollars, up 16.8% year on year. Among them, imports from South Africa and Russia reported the largest growths, up by 50.5% and 16.3% respectively.

1.5.4 Trade protectionism causes certain pressures on the healthy development of the global trade and financial environment

When the economic recovery was not obvious, some countries closed their domestic markets toward foreign countries, provided supports for domestic industries and hindered normal activities of international trade and investment to ease employment pressures. As monitored by WTO, during the period from October 2011 to May 2012, its member countries adopted 182 new trade restrictions to influence 0.9% of global imports. Moreover, the influence of reduced restrictive measures to address the crisis but increased ones to encourage recovery of domestic industries shall be far-reaching. Some countries were conservative toward international investment in emerging industrial areas and even tried to restrict. Catalyzed by electoral politics, some countries even took dangerous trade policies that tend to "deglobalisation".

China became the largest victim of a number of trade protective measures. As monitored by "World Trade Alert", a project of the UK-based Center for Economic Policy Research, after the outbreak of the world financial crisis 2008, around 40% of trade protective measures taken worldwide were against China. As China's export industry is updated from labor-intensive industries to emerging industries, foreign restrictions on exports of China's emerging industries went up significantly. In the first three quarters of 2012, China's exports involved in trade remedy investigations around the world increased by more than 7 times to 24.3 billion dollars. As China's solar photovoltaic batteries encountered trade frictions in a number of oversea markets, exports of this product were heavily hindered[1]. Based on incomplete statistics

---

[1] An Analysis on the Development Environment of China's Foreign Trade in 2013, http://www.cbresearch.com/articledetail/8721.html.

released by the Ministry of Commerce on January 7, 2013, China's exports in 2012 had suffered from 74 trade remedy investigations.

In the face of such severe and complicated situations home and abroad, China also developed a list of corresponding measures to promote further growth of China's foreign trade. In the future, China should make sure that these measures be fully implemented before making full use of the anti-driving mechanism formed by external pressures to prompt enterprises to transform their production modes, elevate their creativity, cultivate new competitive advantages, expand emerging markets and accelerate transformation and update of foreign trade.

1. 6 Forecasts of national economic trends in 2013

1.6.1 Faced with opportunities and risks at the same time, the Chinese economy shall maintain rapid growth in 2013

It can be concluded from the above analysis that industrial structure and regional economic structure in 2012 had no significant change. As China adjusts its enterprise growth pattern and economic structure, its macroeconomic growth is facing challenges. Particularly, the rebounding trend in the global economic environment is still not clear: Though the fiscal cliff of the United States was temporarily relieved, it is still not definite that the United States shall not once again fall off the cliff in 2013. The shadow of Europe's debt crisis is not thoroughly blown off yet. The global political situation remains unstable as in 2011. For domestic economic development: housing prices of the real estate sector that has supported China's rapid economic growth in recent years basically maintained steady in 2012. The slowdown of this growth engine shall cause a ripple effect on relative industries to produce rather obvious impacts on growth rate of the national economy. Influenced by a list of factors, such as rising labor cost, high financing costs of private enterprises, declined demands in the global market, development of private enterprises is faced with huge pressures. State-owned enterprises continue to monopoly the market, which is ill for promoting economic efficiency of the entire society. Rising land cost and labor cost will reduce the attraction of domestic markets to foreign capitals. Therefore, transformation of the economic growth pattern requires a set of supporting policies to provide a room for enterprises to survive while imposing pressures on them.

1.6.2 Income distribution reform shall be further deepened

The long-awaited income distribution reform program was not unveiled in 2012. With the rapid growth of the Chinese economy, it has been a matter of fact that residents' income gap is continuing to widen. Social problems and pressures incurred by this fact will not be revealed when the economy grows up rapidly. However, when the economy slows down, impacts caused by it cannot be neglected. What hides behind the problem is more than the income gap in figures. People already start to study social causes for the gap. More and more attention is given to social problems, such as official bribery, profits of monopoly groups and abnormal gains acquired by rentiers.

Although this strict problem has been widely recognized, it is not an easy job to change it, which has been well illustrated by the delay of the reform program. Information from various channels reveals that vested interest groups are key obstacles in advancing the reform program. The income distribution reform program should be unveiled in 2013. We hope that the program shall play a positive role in pushing forward China's economic, social and political reform and construction.

1.6.3 Of the troika that promote economic growth, consumption shall play a role of increased importance

A vital part of the transformation of the economic growth pattern is the shift from an investment-driven economic growth to a consumption-driven one. This shift has already been manifested in 2012. China's economy had remained under an investment-driven growth pattern, especially a government investment-driven one, for years. Unsustainability of this growth pattern, low efficiency and repeated investment so brought about has become obstacles in the healthy development of the Chinese economy. With the rise of China's national income, it is important in China's economic work to drive up economic growth by stimulating domestic demands. Such key topics as China's current reform of income distribution, cultural development and income doubling program shall actively help stimulate domestic demands.

1.6.4 Under internal and external pressures, it shall be hard to be optimistic about the stock market in 2013

After a slump of 6 years, the stock market showed signs of slight stabilization in the last two months of 2012. Nevertheless, under pressures of worries about domestic and foreign markets, people's market expectations continue to be short of confidence. Though the stock market should be a barometer of national economy, it is not so in China's stock market. Reasons for this phenomenon were complicated. Problems, such as severe information asymmetry, illegal operations, strong speculative atmosphere, speculative behaviors of institutional investors, inadequate punishment and absence of market regulation, are major reasons causing investors to be less confident. Though China Securities Regulatory Commission took a series of measures in 2012 to change the current state of slump, the effect is little. The healthy development of the stock market shall eventually rely on institution construction, particularly implementation of various measures. In whatever areas, we are not in want of laws and regulations. Instead, we are short of powers to execute all provisions of these laws and regulations.

1.6.5 China's import and export shall grow at a low speed

Due to a number of factors, including sluggish demands from the global market when the world economy fails to recover, growing inflationary pressures when all countries tend to enhance easy liquidity, the rise of trade protectionism and rising costs of domestic production, China's foreign trade shall continue to encounter growth pressures in 2013. At the same time, China will also face some opportunities: smooth change of leadership in various countries shall kick off a new round of economic growth; market trades settled in RMB are on the increase; China's domestic economy is gradually stabilizing. All these factors shall combine to determine China's foreign trade in next year. We believe that China's foreign trade shall experience a period of low-speed growth when economic transformation is being advanced and labor cost is on the rise. China's foreign trade can rebound at a high rate only after enterprises successfully elevate their creativity, products are made more competitive and the global economy starts to recover.

References:

1. Statistic database of CEInet, http://db. cei. gov. cn/

2. The database of Wind Info, http://www. wind. com. cn/

3. Statistics of China Customs, http://www. customs. gov. cn/publish/portal0/tab9368/

4. National Bureau of Statistics of China, http://www. stats. gov. cn/

5. An Analysis on the Development Environment of China's Foreign Trade in 2013, http://www. cbresearch. com/articledetail/8721. html.

6. Chen Jiagui and Li Yang, Analysis and Forecasts of China's Economic Situation in 2013, Social Sciences Academic Press, December 2012

7. Report on the Implementation of Central and Local Budgets for 2011 and on Draft Central and Local Budgets for 2012, http://www. gov. cn/2012lh/content_2093446. htm

8. The website of the People's Bank of China, http://www. pbc. gov. cn/

9. The website of China Banking Regulatory Commission, http://www. cbrc. gov. cn/

2 China's Fiscal Revenue in 2012

2.1 A Brief Review of Final Accounts of Fiscal Revenue in 2011

A good start in 2011, the first year of China's "twelfth five-year" planning period, is of great significance toward the successful implementation of the entire "twelfth five-year plan". Faced with serious and complicated economic situations at home and abroad, China continued to implement a proactive fiscal policy and a prudent monetary policy for its macroeconomic regulation and control. Throughout the year, national economy maintained a rapid growth, prices tended to be stable, fiscal revenue was well completed, and civil welfare was further improved, making the year a good start for social and economic development in the "twelfth five-year" planning period.

National revenue totaled 10. 374001 trillion yuan, an increase of 24. 8% over 2010. Breaking them down, central government revenue amounted to 5. 130615 trillion yuan, 111. 9% of the budgeted figure and an increase of 20. 8%. The central budget stabilization fund contributed 150 billion yuan, bringing the total revenue used by the central government to 5. 280615 trillion yuan. The outstanding balance on government bonds in the central budget was 7. 204451 trillion yuan at the end of 2011, which was under the budgeted limit of 7. 770835 trillion yuan for the year. Revenue collected by local governments came to 5. 243386 trillion yuan. Adding the 3. 989996 trillion yuan in tax rebates and transfer payments from the central government, local government revenue totaled 9. 233382 trillion yuan, an increase of 26. 6%.

In 2011, revenue from government-managed funds nationwide came to 4. 135963 trillion yuan, up 12. 4%. Of this figure, receipts from central government-managed funds totaled 312. 593 billion yuan, 110. 6% of the budgeted figure; Revenue collected by local governments from funds under their control reached 3. 82337 trillion yuan, an increase of 13. 8% , including 3. 316624 trillion yuan from the sale of state-owned land use rights.

In 2011, revenue from the state capital operations of the central government totaled 76. 502 billion yuan, 90. 6% of the budgeted figure and an increase of 36. 9% .

As shown in Table 2. 1, Figure 2. 1 and 2. 2, fiscal revenue completed in 2011 had the following characteristics:

(1) Analyzed by the aggregate revenue, fiscal revenue continued to expand in scale with a rapid growth. National revenue in 2011 was 10. 374 trillion yuan (excluding debt revenue), a net growth of more than 2 trillion yuan over the previous year, up 24. 8% and 115. 7% of the budgeted figure at the start of the year. The aggregate fiscal revenue has maintained stable growth since 2001 and increased by 6. 33 times over the past 11 years from 1. 6386 trillion yuan in 2001 to 10. 374 trillion yuan in 2011. Based on percentages of central and local government revenue in national revenue, central government revenue in 2011 made a turn away from the past decade and fell below 50% for the first time.

(2) Based on revenue growth, fiscal revenue grew up at a speed faster than economic growth. Though China's macroeconomic growth declined slightly in 2011, economic growth remained high due to high growth rates in the past several years. China's GDP totaled more than 47 trillion yuan in 2011, a nominal growth of 17. 5% , or a real growth of 9. 2% after deducting price factors. Fiscal revenue in 2011 posted a growth rate close to 25% , faster than GDP growth for the 11th consecutive year since 2001, and was only less than 32. 36% in 2007, but higher than the other 9 years. The proportion of fiscal revenue in GDP climbed up continuously from 14. 94% in 2001 to 22% in 2011.

(3) In light of revenue composition, the proportion of tax revenue was generally on the decline. Tax revenue increased nearly 6 times from 1. 5301 trillion yuan in 2001 to 8. 972 trillion yuan in 2011; non-tax revenue grew up nearly 13 times from 108. 5 billion yuan in 2001 to 1. 402 trillion yuan in 2011, tending to expand continuously when compared to the relative proportion of tax revenue in fiscal revenue. The proportion of tax revenue in fiscal revenue showed a trend of decline year by year except for a slight rebounce in 2010, and hit the bottom of 86. 49% in 2011, indicating that growth of tax revenue failed to catch the overall growth rate of fiscal revenue.

Table 2.1 Fiscal Revenue and Its Growths in 2001～2011

(Unit: 100 million yuan, %)

Year	Fiscal Revenue	Growth rate	Percentage in GDP	GDP Growth rate	Central government revenue			Local governments revenue			Tax revenue	Tax revenue in fiscal revenue
					Revenue	Growth rate	Percentage in total revenue	Revenue	Growth rate	Percentage in total revenue		
2001	16386.04	22.33	14.94	10.52	8582.74	22.80	52.38	7803.3	21.81	47.62	15301	93.38
2002	18903.64	15.36	15.71	9.74	10388.6	21.04	54.96	8515	9.12	45.04	17636	93.3
2003	21715.25	14.87	15.99	12.87	11865.3	14.21	54.64	9849.98	15.68	45.36	20017	92.18
2004	26396.47	21.56	16.51	17.71	14503.1	22.23	54.94	11893.4	20.75	45.06	24166	91.55
2005	31649.29	19.90	17.11	15.67	16548.5	14.10	52.29	15100.8	26.97	47.71	28779	90.93
2006	38760.2	22.47	17.92	16.97	20456.6	23.62	52.78	18303.6	21.21	47.22	34804	89.79
2007	51304.03	32.36	19.31	22.88	27739	35.60	54.07	23565	28.75	45.93	45622	88.92
2008	61330.35	19.54	19.53	18.15	32680.6	17.81	53.29	28649.8	21.58	46.71	54224	88.41
2009	68518.3	11.72	20.12	8.43	35915.7	9.90	52.42	32602.6	13.8	47.58	59522	86.87
2010	83080	21.25	20.69	17.92	42470	18.25	51.12	40610	24.56	48.88	73202	88.11
2011	103740	24.87	22.00	17.45	51306	20.81	49.46	52434	29.12	50.54	89720	86.49

Notes: 1. Central government revenue and local government revenue refer to revenue received respectively by governments at central and local levels, excluding tax rebates and transfer payments from central to local.

2. To keep in line with fiscal revenue and expenditure of the current year, nominal GDP growth rate is calculated based on prices of the current year without adjustment of price indexes.

Source: Calculated based on information from China Statistical Yearbook 2013 and relative information released on the website of the Ministry of Finance.

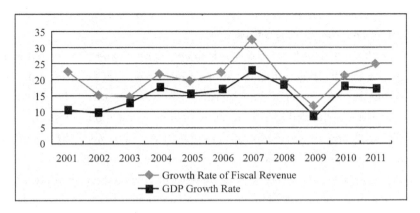

Figure 2. 1 Growth Rates of Fiscal Revenue and GDP Growth Rates in 2001 ~ 2011

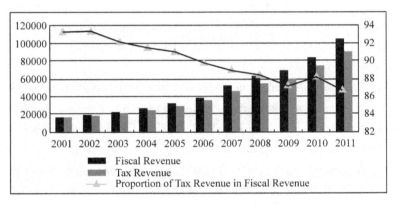

Figure 2. 2 Percentage of Tax Revenue in Fiscal Revenue in 2001 ~ 2011

(4) Based on tax reforms, structural tax reduction was preliminarily implemented. According to the keynote of national macro policies, structural tax reduction has become a significant propeller for boosting transformation of the economic structure and the economic growth pattern. Key tax reform policies launched or initiated in 2011 included: a pilot tax reform program was launched in Shanghai to replace business tax with value-added tax for some industries in order to optimize the industrial structure; the exemption threshold and rates of individual income tax were adjusted to reduce tax burdens on middle-and-low-income citizens; Shanghai and Chongqing launched a pilot property tax program to regulate income distribution; the National People's Congress passed the new vehicle and vessel tax, the reform to impose resource tax

as an ad valorem tax instead of a unit tax to promote energy saving, emission reduction and effective use of resources.

Furthermore, to boost the development of small and micro-sized firms, the policy that the financial and insurance income of rural financial institutions satisfying the requirements shall be subject to business tax at the rate of 3% was extended to the end of 2015; and the policy to halve the corporate income tax for small and micro-sized firms was extended to the end of 2015 and more small and micro-sized firms. To support and increase employment, laid-off people or disable persons engaged in individual operations were entitled to tax reduction or exemption at limited amounts, and enterprises employing laid-off or disable persons were entitled to tax reduction or exemption at fixed rates. To promote regional development, the corporate income tax was imposed at a rate of 15% for enterprises on the list of encouraged industries in Western China; the pilot reform of departure tax rebate and offshore duty-free treatment was launched in Hainan in 2011.

(5) As regards budget management, the dual budget system tended to be perfect. Based on composition of all-inclusive fiscal revenue published by the Ministry of Finance since July 2012, besides fiscal revenue, revenue from government-managed funds and state capital operations of the central government also reported rapid growth. In 2011, revenue from government-managed funds nationwide came to 4. 136313 trillion yuan, up 12. 4%. Receipts from central government-managed funds totaled 313. 082 billion yuan, 110. 8% of the budgeted figure and a decrease of 1. 4%. Revenue collected by local governments from funds under their control reached 3. 823231 trillion yuan, 166. 3% of the budgeted figure and an increase of 13. 8%, including 3. 3477 trillion yuan from the sale of state-owned land use rights[1]. In 2011, revenue

① According to final accounts of local governments-managed funds, revenue from transfer of state-owned land-use rights totaled 3. 31729 trillion yuan, including 70. 709 billion yuan of compensable payments for newly used land, 3. 114042 trillion yuan of sale receipt of state-owned land-use rights, 109. 353 billion yuan of state-owned land return fund, and 23. 186 billion yuan of agricultural and development fund. Revenue from transfer of state-owned land-use rights reflects prices of transactions determined by transferring state-owned land-use rights through bidding, auction, listing, negotiating and allocating, deducting expenditure on costs payable, including compensation for land acquisition and resident relocation.

from the state capital operations of the central government totaled 76. 501 billion yuan, 90. 6% of the budgeted figure and an increase of 36. 9% ①.

2. 2 China's Aggregate Fiscal Revenue in 2012

2. 2. 1 Introduction to the reform of China's fiscal revenue statistic system by Items

Before 2011, classification of China's government revenue and expenditure system was mainly based on Plan for Reform of Classification of Government Revenue and Expenditure becoming effective on January 1, 2007, which was the most significant adjustment of China's classification of government revenue and expenditure system since the founding of the People's Republic of China. Government revenue and expenditure system after the reform is divided into three parts, namely, "classification of revenue", "functional classification of expenditure" and "economic classification of expenditure".

The part "classification of revenue" mainly reflects the nature and source of government revenue. New classification of revenue is no longer included into such items, including general budgetary revenue, budgetary fund revenue and budgetary debt revenue, as required by fund management. Instead, the above revenue is incorporated into a unified revenue classification system by specifically adopting two classification methods, one classified by forms of revenue, such as tax revenue, non-tax revenue, including value-added tax, consumption tax and business tax under tax revenue, and administrative fees, revenue from fines and penalties under non-tax revenue, to accounting for the way in which revenue is collected; and the other classified by source, some classified by ownership, like value-added tax on state-owned enterprises and collective ones under value-added tax, some classified by sectors, like cultural administrative fees and public security administrative fees under administrative fees, cultural fines and penalties, and public security fines and penalties under fines and penalties, to explain where the revenue is from.

---

① After restructuring state-owned enterprises and the reform of restructuring major enterprises and relaxing control over small ones, central enterprises are basically the major part, so the central public finance set up a budget for state capital operations. However, proceeds of state capital operations of local governments in 2011 were not listed independently, usually included in the public finance budget.

After the reform, fiscal revenue is classified into the following categories and items:

(1) Tax revenue, including 23 items: value-added tax, consumption tax, business tax, corporate income tax, rebates for corporate income tax, individual income tax, resource tax, tax on adjustment of the orientation of investment in fixed assets, urban construction and maintenance taxes, house property tax, stamp tax, urban land use tax, land appreciation tax, vehicle and vessel tax, vessel tonnage tax, vehicle purchase tax, livestock slaughter tax, banquet tax, customs duties, farmland occupation tax, deed tax, and other tax revenues.

(2) Revenue of social insurance funds, including 6 items: revenue of basic pension funds, revenue of unemployment insurance funds, revenue of basic medical insurance funds, revenue of work-related injury insurance funds, revenue of maternity insurance funds and revenue of other social insurance funds.

(3) Non-tax revenue, including 8 items: revenue from government-managed funds, special revenue, lottery revenue, revenue from fines and penalties, revenue from operations of state-owned capital, revenue from paid use of state-owned resources (assets), and revenue from other sources.

(4) Income from principal recovered from loans and re-lending, including: income from principal recovered from domestic loans, income from principal recovered from foreign loans, income from principal recovered from domestic re-lending and income from principal recovered from foreign re-lending.

(5) Debt revenue, including domestic debt revenue and foreign debt revenue.

(6) Transfer income, including: rebate, transfer payments, special transfer payment, transfer of government-managed funds, transfer of lottery proceed funds, subsidies of social insurance funds, transfer of extra-budgetary funds, transfer between units, balance revenue of last year, transferred capital.

In June 2010, the Ministry of Finance issued the "Circular on Bringing Revenue Managed as Extrabudgetary Funds into the Budget", deciding to bring nationwide revenue managed as extrabudgetary funds into the budget since January 1, 2011, so that revenue is turned over in full to Treasury and expenditure is arranged through public finance budget or budget for government-managed funds. Local finances at all levels are required by the State Council to bring revenue managed as extrabudgetary funds into the budget since January 1, 2011. *Classification of Government Revenue and Expenditure Items* was correspondingly revised and all extrabudgetary revenue and expenditure items were removed.

By centering around the management of separating revenue from expenditure, China initiated the reform on management of extra-budgetary funds, putting administrative and institutional charges, fines and penalties that belong to general budgetary revenue under the public finance budget, to be arranged and used together with tax revenue; putting government-managed funds, income from land transfer and lottery proceeds that feature "expenditure determined by revenue and special fund for special use" under the budget for government-managed funds, to be used for construction of special infrastructure and development of social programs. Through the above measures, the size of extra-budgetary funds has been effectively controlled. Since 2011, all government revenue managed as extra-budgetary funds was brought into the budget, indicating that extra-budgetary funds have become a matter of history.

The overall removal of extra-budgetary funds and putting all government revenue and expenditure under the management of budgets is an important milestone in the reform of China's budget management system and even in the reform of China's fiscal regime, has achieved remarkable results and is of great significance. First, make distribution of government funds more standard, ensure complete budgets and promote construction of a government budget system that is organically composed of public finance budgets, budget for government-managed funds, budget for state capital operations and budget for social insurance funds. Second, bring the economic order back to normal and is good to reduce adverse activities, such as arbitrary charges, fines and apportions to treat corruption from the source. Third, intensify management of financial funds, making it easier for the People's Congress and all walks of life to supervise, improving transparency of public finance management and legal financing. According to a preliminary calculation, about 6 billion yuan of the central government and 250 billion yuan of local governments that were originally managed as extra-budgetary funds were put under the budget in 2011[①].

The 18th National Congress of the Communist Party of China began on November 8, 2012. The Report to the Eighteenth National Congress of the Communist Party of China clearly vows to "tighten examination and oversight of all government budgets and final accounts". This means that all government revenue and expenditure should be examined and overseen by the People's Congress. After putting all revenue and expenditure under budgets, the People's Congress shall not only pay attention to final accounts of the public finance. At least the budget for state capital operations, the budget for government-managed funds, the budget for social insurance funds and their final accounts should be submitted to the People's Congress for audit and supervision as regulated by the law. The draft of budget law that is currently under revision also clearly puts forward that China's budget system should be complicated one, including public finance budget, budget for government-managed funds, budget for state capital operations and budget for social insurance funds", with stresses on the unity and integrity of budget preparation.

2.2.2 Budget for fiscal revenue in 2012[②]

Considering that China's economic development may face a more complex situation in 2012, and that there may be a significant imbalance between revenue and expenditure, the Chinese government was prudent in arranging revenue growth target in its budgetary report published at the start of 2012. The following major targets were set for the 2012 fiscal budget:

(1) Major targets for the fiscal budget

As for the budget of the central government, central government revenue shall reach 5.592 trillion yuan, an increase of 9% over the actual figure for 2011 (here and below). Adding the 270 billion yuan from the central budget stabilization fund, disposable revenue for 2012 should amount to 5.862 tril-

---

① Xinhua. net: The Ministry of Finance: Above 250 Million Extra-budgetary Funds Incorporated under Supervision, May 18, 2012, http://finance. jrj. com. cn/2012/05/18200513185770. shtml

② The following data are mainly from Report on the Implementation of Central and Local Budgets for 2011 and on Draft Central and Local Budgets for 2012 (Summary), released on March 5, 2012 on the website of the Ministry of Finance.

lion yuan. Central government expenditure should total 6.412 trillion yuan, an increase of 13.7%. This consists of 1.8519 trillion yuan incurred at the central level, up 12.1%; 4.5101 trillion yuan paid out as tax rebates and transfer payments to local governments, up 13%; and 50 billion yuan used as reserve funds in the central budget, the same as the budgeted figure for 2011. Expenditure exceeds revenue in the central budget, leaving a deficit of 550 billion yuan, down 100 billion. The ceiling for the outstanding balance on government bonds in the central budget stands at 8.270835 trillion yuan.

As for budgets of local governments, based on preliminary provisions for local budgets compiled by the central government, revenue collected by local governments will amount to 5.768 trillion yuan, an increase of 10%. Adding the 4.5101 trillion yuan in tax rebates and transfer payments from the central government, local government revenue will total 10.2781 trillion yuan. The central government will issue 250 billion yuan worth of treasury bonds for local governments, an increase of 50 billion yuan over the previous year.

Combining central and local budgets, national revenue will be 11.36 trillion yuan, up 9.5%. Adding the 270 billion yuan from the central budget stabilization fund, total available national revenue is projected to be 11.63 trillion yuan. Total national expenditure is budgeted at 12.43 trillion yuan, up 14.1%. Total expenditure exceeds total revenue by 800 billion yuan (including the 550 billion yuan central government deficit), 50 billion yuan less than last year and bringing the deficit down to approximately 1.5% of GDP.

In 2012, the following targets were set for major revenue items in the central budget: revenue from domestic VAT will amount to 2.025 trillion yuan, up 10.8%; revenue from domestic excise tax, 770 billion yuan, up 11%; revenue from customs duties as well as VAT and excise tax on imports, 1.7528 trillion yuan, up 8.7%; revenue from corporate income tax, 1.112 trillion yuan, up 11%; revenue from individual income tax, 340 billion yuan, down 6.4%; VAT and excise tax rebates on exports, 995 billion yuan, up 8.1%; and non-tax revenue, 282.6 billion yuan, up 5.6%.

Targets for central government tax rebates and transfer payments: Central government tax rebates and transfer payments to local governments will amount to 4.5101 trillion yuan, up 13%. This figure consists of 518.855 billion yuan in tax rebates, up 2.2%; 2.252619 trillion yuan in general transfer payments, up 23.1%; and 1.738626 trillion yuan in special transfer payments, up 5.2%.

(2) Budgets for government-managed funds

Revenue from central government-managed funds will total 299.035 billion yuan, down 4.3%. Adding the 81.731 billion yuan of revenue carried forward from last year, total disposable revenue from central government-managed funds will be 380.766 billion yuan. Revenue collected through local government-managed funds will reach 3.180641 trillion yuan, down 16.8%. Adding the 131.033 billion yuan in transfer payments from central government-managed funds, revenue from local government-managed funds will amount to 3.311674 trillion yuan.

Combined revenue from funds managed by central and local governments will reach 3.479676 trillion yuan, down 15.9%. Adding the 81.731 billion yuan carried forward from last year, available revenue from government-managed funds will total 3.561407 trillion yuan.

(3) Budgets for State Capital Operations

In 2012, revenue from the central government's state capital operations will reach 84.4 billion yuan, up 10.3%. Revenue from local governments' state capital operations will total 40.249 billion yuan. Adding up central and local governments' budgetary appropriations, total revenue from state capital operations will be 124.649 billion yuan, and adding the 3.107 billion yuan carried forward from last year, disposable revenue will amount to 127.756 billion yuan. Total expenditure on state capital operations will reach 127.756 billion yuan.

2.2.3 Implementation of Fiscal Revenue in 2012

(1) Government revenue

In 2012, national revenue totaled 11.7210 trillion yuan, an increase of 1.3335 trillion yuan, or 12.8%. Breaking down, central government revenue amounted to 5.6133 trillion yuan, an increase of 480.5 billion yuan or 9.4%; the revenue of local governments came to 6.1077 trillion yuan, a growth of 853 billion yuan or 16.2%. Of the total fiscal revenue, tax revenue reached 10.0601 trillion yuan, up 12.1%.

Throughout the year, the annual growth rate of national fiscal revenue was 12.2 percentage points lower than the 2011 level, and that of tax revenue

10. 5 percentage points lower. The major factors contributing to the significant cut in fiscal revenue included softening domestic economy, weakening corporate profits, milder inflation—especially the drop in producer price as well as structural tax breaks.

(2) Revenue of government-managed funds

In 2012, revenue of government-managed funds nationwide totaled 3. 7517 trillion yuan, 384. 6 billion yuan less than the same period of last year, or a decline of 9. 3%. Of this total, receipts of central government-managed funds reached 331. 3 billion yuan, a growth of 18. 3 billion yuan, or 5. 8%; revenue of funds managed by local governments came to 3. 4204 trillion yuan, a decrease of 402. 9 billion yuan, or 10. 5%, mainly due to reduced turnover of land transfer. Receipts from transfer of state-owned land use rights were 2. 8517 trillion yuan, a decrease of 465. 6 billion, or 14%.

2.2.4 General Trend of Fiscal Revenue in 2012 and it's Major Factors

Based on the trend of fiscal revenue, growth of fiscal revenue in the first three quarters of 2012 declined quarter after quarter, while showing a pattern of gradual declining and rebounding in the last quarter. To be specific, fiscal revenue rose up by 14. 7% in Quarter 1, 10% in Quarter 2, reduced to 8. 1% in Quarter 3 and grew up by 19.9% in Quarter 4.

In the first three quarters of 2012, the growth of national revenue was down by 18. 6 percentage points from that in the same period of last year; of the total growth, the growth of tax revenue was down by 18. 8 percentage points year on year. The sharp decline of revenue growth in the first three quarters was a comprehensive reflection of economic slowdown, reduced growth of enterprise profits, sluggish growths of imports and implementation of the structural tax reduction policy. To be specific, major reasons were as follows:

First, economic growth slowed down and enterprise profits reduced. In the first three quarters, GDP growth calculated at comparable prices increased by 7. 7% year on year (10% if calculated at current prices), down by 1. 7 percentage points; the value added of industrial enterprises above the designated size increased by 10% (9. 2% in September), down 4. 2 percentage points; investment in fixed assets was up by 20. 5% over the previous year, down by 4.4 percentage points; the total retail sales of consumer goods grew up by 14.1% over the previous year, 2.9 percentage points lower than the same period of last year; general trade import was up by 3.6%, down 29.7 percentage points; sales of commercial housing increased by 2.7%, down 20.5 percentage points. The profits made by the industrial enterprises above the designated size in the first nine months decreased by 1.8%, down by 28.8 percentage points year on year. Correspondingly, growth of tax items such as value-added tax, business tax, tax on imports, corporate income tax declined sharply.

Second, price growth declined. In the first three quarters, the consumer price went up by 2.8%, down 2.9 percentage points from that in the same period of last year, particularly the producer prices that decreased by 1.5% year on year, down by 8.5 percentage points. Growth of revenue from turn-over taxes calculated at current prices was correspondingly down.

Third, great efforts were made through the policy of structural tax reduction. In 2012, China continued to implement the policy of structural tax reduction that aimed to adjust income distribution, support the development of small and micro-sized firms, adjust the industrial structure, expand exports and stabilize prices. Correspondingly, revenue from tax items covered by the policy was down, including individual income tax, corporate income tax, value-added tax, business tax and customs duties.

Main reasons for the growth of fiscal revenue to go up in Quarter 4 included: First, the rebounce of macroeconomic growth boosted the growth of relative tax revenue. Growths of main economic indicators, including the value added of the industrial sector, the total retail sales of consumer goods, investment in fixed assets and profits made by the industrial enterprises, correspondingly drove up growths of value-added tax, business tax and corporate income tax. Second, due to the economic downturn in the same period of last year, growth of fiscal revenue drastically reduced since October 2011, particularly in the last two months of 2011, in which the revenue base was so low as to cause revenue growth rate in Quarter 4 of 2012 relatively high.

2. 3 Structure of China's Fiscal Revenue in 2012

2.3.1 Monthly Structure of Fiscal Revenue

In general, national revenue in 2012 posted a growth much less than that in the same period of last year. National revenue in the first 11 months totaled 10.8903 trillion yuan, a growth of 1.1594 trillion yuan over last year, or up 11.9%. Specific monthly growths are shown in Table 2.2 and Figure 2.3:

Table 2.2 National Fiscal Revenue and its Growth in 2012

(Unit: 100 million yuan)

Month	National revenue in 2012	Central government revenue	Local government revenue	National revenue in 2011	Year-on-Year Growth	Year-on-Year Growth rate
1	12912.58	6413.76	6498.82	11497.38	1415.2	12.3%
2	8005.7	4192.6	3813.1	6997.01	1008.69	14.4%
3	9057.97	4036.14	5021.83	7631.35	1426.62	18.7%
4	10774	5477	5297	10082.06	692.06	6.9%
5	12005	6991	5014	10612.26	1392.74	13.1%
6	11040	4709	6331	10055.76	984.24	9.8%
7	10672	5562	5110	9864.1	807.9	8.2%
8	7863	3765	4098	7546.37	316.63	4.2%
9	8258	3664	4594	7377.05	880.95	11.9%
10	10444	5119	5325	9188.34	1255.66	13.7%
11	7871	3672	4199	6457.32	1413.68	21.9%
12	8307	2532	5775	6566	1741	26.5%
Total	117210	56133	61077	103875	13335	12.8%

Notes: Revenue data in December 2011 and December 2012 are obtained through calculation based on the totals in both years. Total revenue of 2011 adopts the final account of 2011.

Source: Calculated and compiled based on data from the data center of CEInet and the website of the Ministry of Finance.

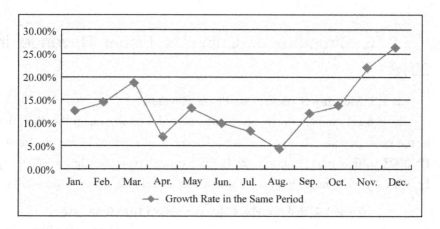

Figure 2. 3 Year-on-year Growth of National Revenue in 2012

As for monthly growth, in contrast to the declining trend of fiscal revenue growth in 2011, the growth rate of national revenue in 2012 showed
quite an opposite trend that "dropped month after month and rebounded in
late 2012", except for a sharp decline in April. In the first 10 months, the
growth rate of national revenue reached the peak at 18. 4% in March and
then turned to decline all the way to the bottom at 4. 2% in August. After
that, it picked up gradually and later largely to above 20% in November and
December.

As shown by monthly data of fiscal revenue, attention should be paid to
the following aspects:

(1) In Quarter 1, national revenue totaled 2. 997625 trillion yuan, a
growth of 385. 051 billion yuan over the same period of last year, up 14. 7%.
Of this total, tax revenue stood for 2. 585781 trillion yuan, up 10. 3%. Non-
tax revenue posted 411. 8 billion yuan, a gain of 143. 2 billion yuan, up
53. 3%. Of total non-tax revenue, that collected by local governments amounted to 347. 2 billion yuan, an increase of 115. 8 billion yuan, up 50. 1%,
mainly because part of non-tax revenue at the end of last year was turned over
into Treasury at the start of 2012 and some places enhanced collection of non-
tax revenue.

(2) Fiscal revenue reduced in growth in April mainly because income taxes and tax on imports declined sharply. The growth of corporate income tax was only 2.5%, 18% lower than the previous three quarters, mainly affected by dropped profits realized by enterprises and the factor of structural tax cuts. Individual income tax was 13.8% lower than that in the same period of last year, and 7.6% lower than the previous three quarters, mainly affected by the raised threshold for individual income tax on wages and salaries and the adjusted tax rates for self-employed industrial and commercial households, both of which reduced the revenue. Value-added tax and consumption tax on imports totaled 114.2 billion yuan, down 2.3%, but customs duties was up 0.5%, respectively down 15.3% and 9.1% from the previous three quarters, mainly affected by the slowdown of general trade imports and the factor of structural tax cuts implemented on some imports.

(3) In August, national revenue reached 786.3 billion yuan, an increase of 31.7 billion yuan or 4.2% over the same period of last year. Of this total, central government revenue was 376.5 billion yuan, down 6.7% year on year; local government revenue totaled 409.8 billion yuan, up 16.8%. Tax revenue amounted to 661.8 billion yuan, up 7.2%. Revenue growth dropped substantially in this month, especially the central government revenue that declined dramatically, mainly affected by slowed economic growth, reduced price increases, dropped enterprise profits and structural tax cuts implemented, in addition to incomparable factors, such as the new method adopted for special petroleum proceeds paid into the treasury and rebates for corporate income tax of last year and next year.

(4) Fiscal revenue picked up slightly in growth since September, especially in the last three months. Main reasons were as stated in the above: First, economic growth rebounded to boost the growth of relative tax revenue. Second, due to the economic downturn in Quarter 4 of 2011, growth of fiscal revenue drastically reduced since October 2011, particularly in the last two months of 2011, in which the revenue base was so low as to cause revenue growth rate in Quarter 4 of 2012 relatively high.

2.3.2 Analysis of fiscal revenue by provinces

National revenue in 2012 totaled 11.721 trillion yuan. Of this total, central government revenue amounted to 5.6133 trillion yuan, a growth of 480.5

billion yuan, or 9.4% ; local government revenue amounted to 6.1077 trillion yuan, a rise of 853 billion yuan, or 16.2%. Based on composition of fiscal revenue, revenue from tax on imports, value-added tax, individual income tax, vehicle purchase tax, and stamp tax on security transactions that were completely or largely attributable to central government revenue received a low growth or was on the decline, particularly export tax rebates currently paid out by the central government in full, which grew up largely to reduce the revenue. All these affected the growth of central government revenue. Revenue from business tax, which are mainly assigned to local governments, other tax items levied by local governments, and non-tax revenue of local governments grew up rapidly to boost the growth of local revenue. Correspondingly, the growth of central government revenue was lower than that of local government revenue.

Based on fiscal revenue of all local governments, growths of fiscal revenue in 2012 were down slightly from 2011. Table 2.3 shows completion and growth rates of fiscal revenue in all regions. Fiscal revenue completed by all provincial governments in 2012 had the following two basic features: 1. Based on the absolute figures of fiscal revenue in the first ten months of 2012, Guangdong Province had the highest revenue of above 500 billion yuan while Tibet had the lowest of only 5.1 billion yuan, the former equal to more than 100 times of the latter. Of all provinces, regions and municipals, 21 provinces, regions and municipals collected more than 100 billion yuan of fiscal revenue, and the remaining 10 provinces, regions and municipals received less than 100 billion yuan. 2. Based on growths of fiscal revenue received by all local governments in 2012, Jiangxi and Guizhou had the largest growth rates of above 30% , but Shannxi posted a negative growth of 5.6% , mainly because growth rates of fiscal revenue in all areas were excessively high in the same period of last year. Of all areas, 20 provinces, regions and municipals had a growth rate exceeding or equal to 15.8% , the growth rate of total local revenue, but the remaining 11 provinces, regions and municipals had a rate below that.

Table 2.3 Fiscal Revenue of All Provinces (Autonomous Regions and Municipals) in January to October of 2012   (Unit: 100 million yuan, %)

No.	Province	Public finance revenue	Growth rate in first 10 months of 2012	Growth rate in 2011	Percentage in the total of local government revenue
1	Beijing	2886.3	9.7	27.7	5.65
2	Tianjin	1477.8	23.5	36.1	2.89
3	Hebei	1754.9	18.5	27.6	3.43
4	Liaoning	2645.9	21.6	31.7	5.18
5	Shanghai	3392.5	9.0	19.4	6.64
6	Jiangsu	4843.2	14.5	26.2	9.48
7	Zhejiang	3063.1	7.3	20.8	5.99
8	Fujian	1468.5	17.9	30.4	2.87
9	Shandong	3488.5	17.3	25.69	6.83
10	Guangdong	5186.9	11.6	22.1	10.15
11	Hainan	344.3	20.0	25.5	0.67
12	Shanxi	1310.5	22.0	25.12	2.56
13	Jilin	863.6	20.6	41.1	1.69
14	Heilongjiang	953.7	15.6	32	1.87
15	Anhui	1507.6	24.0	27.3	2.95
16	Jiangxi	1157.9	33.8	35.4	2.27
17	Henan	1689.5	17.0	24.6	3.31
18	Hubei	1435.3	22.1	45.4	2.81
19	Hunan	1416.2	21.6	34.6	2.77
20	Shannxi	1219.1	−5.6	56.5	2.39
21	Guizhou	835.2	33.7	44.9	1.63
22	Ningxia	220.5	15.8	42	0.43
23	Tibet	51.0	17.1	49.2	0.10
24	Xinjiang	718.5	24.2	44	1.41
25	Qinghai	159.7	20.6	37.7	0.31

(**Continued**)

No.	Province	Public finance revenue	Growth rate in first 10 months of 2012	Growth rate in 2011	Percentage in the total of local government revenue
26	Gansu	431. 2	14. 8	27. 4	0. 84
27	Sichuan	1961. 1	17. 3	30. 9	3. 76
28	Chongqing	1319. 4	15. 4	46. 2	2. 58
29	Inner Mongolia	1261. 0	9. 4	27	2. 47
30	Yunnan	1099. 5	20. 3	27. 5	2. 15
31	Guangxi	921. 4	20. 7	22. 7	1. 80
	Total	51103. 8	15. 8		100

Source: Data obtained based on relative information published on the website of the Ministry of Finance and Progress Database 2012 of the National Bureau of Statistics of China.

2.3.3 Analysis of fiscal revenue by categories and items

From the beginning of 2011, China started to implement the reformed budget management system, incorporating the original extra-budgetary funds (excluding education charges) into the budget management. However, as the actual implementation differed in all provinces and municipals, only some provinces and regions did bring all extra-budgetary funds under budget management. National expenditure and revenue were required to be brought under the budget since 2012, and extra-budgetary funds became a part of history.

Based on the integrity of the budget system, budgets and final accounts of governments at various levels should include budgets for government revenue and expenditure, state capital operations, government-managed funds and social security. Except for the budget for social security that has not been published, the first three budgets were published on the website of the Ministry of Finance. As for categories of fiscal revenue, based on their coverage from big to small, we shall analyze percentages of the first three kinds of revenue in total fiscal revenue, percentages of tax revenue and non-tax revenue in government revenue, and percentages of all tax items in tax revenue.

(1) Structure of fiscal revenue by categories

Analyzed by the aggregate revenue, national revenue totaled 10. 1032 trillion yuan in the first ten months and 11. 721 trillion yuan in the full year.

Among the total, revenue from operation of state-owned capital was 150. 49 billion yuan, revenue from paid use of state-owned resources (assets) amounted to 237. 76 billion yuan, and both added up to 388. 25 billion yuan, around 3. 84% of total budgetary revenue[1]. According to the growth rates, in the first ten months of 2012, national budgetary revenue rose up by 11. 2% from that in the same period of last year, while revenue from operation of state-owned capital had a growth of 28. 6% year on year, and revenue from paid use of state-owned resources (assets) a gain of 64. 7%, both far above the growth rate of public finance revenue.

Throughout the year of 2012, national revenue from government-managed funds totaled 3. 7517 trillion yuan, accounting for 32% of total national revenue, down 384. 6 billion yuan or 9. 3% from the same period of last year. Of this total, revenue from central government-managed funds amounted to 331. 3 billion yuan, up 18. 3 billion yuan or 5. 8% year on year; that from local governments-managed funds was 3. 4204 trillion yuan, down 402. 9 billion yuan or 10. 5%, mainly caused by largely reduced turnover of land transfer. Revenue from transfer of the right to use state-owned lands reached 2. 8517 trillion yuan, a decrease of 465. 6 billion yuan or 14% year on year.

(2) Structure of tax revenue and non-tax revenue in fiscal revenue

Analyzed by the aggregate revenue, national revenue in 2012 totaled 11. 721 trillion yuan. Of this total, tax revenue amounted to 10. 0601 trillion yuan, standing for 85. 8% of total national revenue; non-tax revenue was 1. 42405 trillion, 14. 1%. Viewed by revenue growth rate, national revenue in 2012 rose up by 12. 8% year on year. Of the total growth, tax revenue posted a growth of 12. 1% while non-tax revenue a rise of 17. 5%, making significant contributions to the growth of fiscal revenue as a whole.

Growth of tax revenue in 2012 presented the following characteristics: First, the growth rate of total tax revenue reduced remarkably and hit the bottom in the past 3 years, respectively 10. 5 and 10. 9 percentage points below that of 2011 and 2010. Second, analyzed by quarters, the growth rate of tax revenue showed a trend of slow decline in the first three quarters and then

---

[1] Though revenue of state capital operations is in parallel to government revenue in the budget, it was still put under government revenue in actual statistics of 2012 because its amount was too small.

picked up slightly in Quarter 4. Third, growth rates of major tax types dropped sharply. Domestic value-added tax, business tax and corporate income tax respectively grew up by 8.9%, 15.1% and 17.2% year on year, down 6.1%, 7.5% and 13.4%. Fourth, revenue from individual income tax reduced significantly. Data showed that individual income tax in 2012 reduced by 3.9% year on year, a drop of 29.1 percentage points from that of the previous year. Of the total reduction, tax on income from wages and salaries and income from production or business operation of individual industrial and commercial households decreased drastically by 8% and 12.5% respectively.

Based on non-tax revenue received by governments at various levels, non-tax revenue of the central government was 284.9 billion yuan, a gain of 5.7%; that of local governments was 1.376 trillion yuan, a lift of 20.3%. Major reasons for the large growth of non-tax revenue of local government were as follows: First, as extra-budgetary revenue was required to be brought into the budget 2011, some places initiated relative work at the beginning of the year, causing the base of non-tax revenue in Quarter 1 of 2011 to be relatively low. At the same time, part of non-tax revenue in 2011 were cleaned up and turned into Treasury at the beginning of 2012, which correspondingly caused non-tax revenue of local governments in Quarter 1 of 2012 to largely grew up by 115.8 billion yuan year on year, about half of the total growth in the full year. Second, local government enhanced efforts on levying and collecting payment for use of state-owned resources (assets). Revenue from such payment registered a growth of 95.5 billion yuan over last year, approximately 40% in the growth of non-tax revenue of local governments.

Based on internal composition of non-tax revenue, non-tax revenue in the first ten months of 2012 totaled 1.42405 trillion yuan. Of this total, special revenue was 252.39 billion yuan, accounting for 17.17% of total non-tax revenue; revenue from administrative fees was 379.62 billion yuan, 26.7%; revenue from fines and penalties stood at 126.82 billion yuan, 8.9%; revenue from operation of state-owned capital was 150.49 billion yuan and that from paid use of state-owned resources (assets) 237.76 billion yuan, both added up to accounting for 27.3%; and non-tax revenue from other sources totaled 276.97 billion yuan, 19.4%.

(3) Analysis on taxes and variation of tax revenue

Based on the nature of tax objectives, the structure of tax regime can generally be divided into tax on goods (or services), tax on income and tax on property. According to China's tax law system, taxes usually fall into five categories, namely, turnover tax, income tax, resource tax, property tax and act tax, totaling above 20 items. Table 2.4 presents a brief summary of China's taxes mainly based on their revenue scale and growth, contributions to and percentages of tax revenue.

Table 2.4 National Tax Revenue and Revenue of Major Taxes in 2012

(Unit: 100 million yuan;%)

Category	Tax item	January to December 2012			2012		
		Total revenue	Year-on-year Growth rate	Proportion in tax revenue	Total revenue	Year-on-year Growth	Year-on-year Growth rate
Goods and services tax	Domestic value-added tax	21440.0	6.2	24.7	26415.69	2149.06	8.9
	Domestic consumption tax	6811.6	11.6	7.8	7872.69	935.93	13.5
	Value-added tax and consumption tax on imports	12160.2	2.9	14.0	14796.41	1235.99	9.1
	Rebates of value-added tax and consumption tax on exports	−8414.2	15.3	−9.7	−10428.88	−1224.13	13.3
	customs duties	2309.5	4.0	2.6	2782.74	223.62	8.7
	business tax	13162.0	13.1	15.1	15747.53	2068.53	15.1
	urban construction and maintenance taxes	2607.4	11.6	3.0	3126	347.33	12.5
	stamp tax	834.0	−6.4	1.0	/	/	/
	stamp tax on stock trading	267.8	−30.9	0.3	303.52	−134.93	−30.8
	resource tax	773.9	57.6	0.9	/	/	/
	vehicle purchase tax	1830.0	10.7	2.1	2228.27	183.38	9.0
	Tobacco tax	91.7	54.2	0.1	/	/	/
	Subtotal	53873.9	/	62.0	/	/	/

Category	Tax item	January to December 2012			2012		
		Total revenue	Year-on-year Growth rate	Proportion in tax revenue	Total revenue	Year-on-year Growth	Year-on-year Growth rate
Income tax	corporate income tax	19587.0	15.2	22.5	19653.56	2883.92	17.2
	individual income tax	4960.2	−7.2	5.7	5820.24	−233.87	−3.9
	land appreciation tax	2217.5	25.8	2.5	2718.84	656.23	31.8
	Subtotal	26764.7	/	30.7	/	/	/
Property tax	house property tax	1174.9	24.5	1.3	1372.49	270.10	24.5
	farmland occupation tax	1270.1	56.9	1.46	1621	545.35	50.7
	urban land use tax	1314.4	26.3	1.5	1541.72	319.46	26.1
	vehicle and vessel tax	327.6	28.5	0.4	/	/	/
	vessel tonnage tax	34.1	40.2	0.04	/	/	/
	deed tax	2296.2	−1.5	2.6	2873.92	108.19	3.9
	Subtotal	6417.3	/	7.3	/	/	/
	Total tax revenue	86791.6	9.0	100	100600.88	10862.49	12.1

Notes: Data for minor tax items in the full year of 2012, such as stamp tax, resource tax, tobacco tax, vehicle and vessel tax, vessel tonnage tax was currently unavailable.

Source: Sorted based on relative information taken from the website of the Ministry of Finance and Progressive Database 2012 of the National Bureau of Statistics of China.

As for the structure of tax regime in 2012, in general, data given in the above table indicate that: On one side, China's tax regime continued to be dominated by turnover taxes. In the first ten months of 2012, goods and services tax totaled 5.38739 trillion yuan, accounting for 62% of tax revenue; income tax amounted to 2.67647 trillion yuan, accounting for 30.7%; and property tax reached 641.73 billion yuan, 7.3%. In the following, we make a brief analysis of changes to major taxes:

First, revenue from domestic value-added tax in 2012 was 2.641569 trillion yuan, up 8.9% year on year, or above 6 percentage points below that of last year, accounting for 26.2% of total tax revenue.

Second, revenue from domestic consumption tax in 2012 was 787.214 trillion yuan, up 13.5% year on year, roughly the same as the previous year, accounting for 7.8% of total tax revenue.

Third, revenue from value-added tax and consumption tax on imports totaled 1.479641 trillion yuan, up 9.1% year on year, or down 20.2 percentage points from last year, accounting for 14.7% of total tax revenue.

Fourth, revenue from business tax totaled 1.574753 trillion yuan, up 15.1% year on year, or down 7.5 percentage points from last year, accounting for 15.6% of total tax revenue.

Fifth, revenue from corporate income tax totaled 1.965356 trillion yuan, up 17.2% year on year, or down 13.4 percentage points from last year, accounting for 19.5% of total tax revenue. In addition, of revenue from corporate income tax, 509.838 billion yuan of corporate income tax of 2011 was settled and paid in 2012, a growth of 102.234 billion yuan or 25.1%, accounting for nearly 40% of the growth of corporate income tax; prepaid corporate income tax for 2012 was up by 8.4%, 21.6 percentage points lower than that in the previous year.

Sixth, revenue from individual income tax totaled 582.034 billion yuan, down 3.9% year on year, or 29.1 percentage points from last year, a negative growth that appeared for the first time. By items, income tax on? income from production or business operation conducted by self-employed industrial and commercial households and income tax on wages and salaries declined substantially, down by 12.5% and 8% respectively; income tax on interest, dividends and bonuses, income tax on remuneration for providing services, and income tax on income from transfer of property increased by 14.7%, 10.8% and 6.5% respectively.

In general, the growth of tax revenue in 2012 sharply dropped from the previous year, which comprehensively reflected the slowdown of economic growth, declined enterprise profits, sluggish import growth and implementation of structural tax reduction.

First, on the macroeconomic aspect, increasingly tightened economic situations home and abroad was the root cause for tax revenue growth to fall down.

As tax revenue is a major part of fiscal revenue, its growth is closely connected with the economic situations. Usually, the size of economic tax sources is determined by GDP size. After deducting price factors, tax revenue was basically synchronous with GDP growth. As analyzed in Chapter 1, the growth of industrial added value, total retail sales of consumer goods, and the growth of profits achieved by industrial enterprises above the designated size in China declined in 2012. At the same time, the sharp drop of prices caused tax revenue growth calculated at present prices to decline. What's more, the general trade export experienced a large reduction. All these factors combined to result in considerable impacts on tax revenue.

As for value-added tax, its tax base was reduced because industrial added value fell down in growth and prices continued to decline. As the economic growth slowed down, demand for and prices of basic raw material were on the decline, causing revenue from value-added tax in relative sectors to reduce. As international oil prices continued to rise in early 2012, prices of oil bought by petroleum processing enterprises were relatively high, which reduced value added in refined oil.

Second, on the microeconomic aspect, development of various sectors and industries had direct influences on some specific taxes.

For domestic consumption tax, its tax base is formed by the sales of 14 special products, including tobacco, win, automobiles and refined oil. Since the beginning of 2012, tobacco output was slow in growth, production of white spirit and sales of valuable jewelry remained on the rise, so that consumption tax maintained a steady growth in general. As the tax base of value-added tax and consumption tax on imports falls on general trade imports, revenue from value-added tax and consumption tax on imports reduced in 2012 because the growth of China's general trade imports reduced by nearly 30% year on year and imports of some key products, such as crude oil and steel, saw sharp decline in growth or negative growth.

For business tax, except for the sector of banking, business tax in sectors, including transportation, construction, real estate, leasing and business services, reported drops in growths, mainly because: sales of commercial housing reduced in growth, causing revenue from business tax on real estates to fall down; and investment in construction was down in growth, resulting in decline in business tax in the sector of construction.

As for corporate income tax, of 20 key industrial sectors, corporate income tax of above 50% of sectors declined. In particular, the growth of corporate income tax saw sharp declines in sectors of refined oil, steel billet and textile, and slight drops in the remaining sectors, mainly caused by reduced profits made by industrial enterprises. Of 41 industrial sectors, profits of 10 sectors were down year on year and 1 sector was in the red, which affected revenue from prepaid corporate income tax. Furthermore, the market of second-hand houses was thin and transaction prices fell down, causing income tax on property transfer to reduce correspondingly.

Third, based on tax policies and levying management, structural tax cut policies had substantial impacts on the decline of tax revenue.

China raise the threshold for value-added tax and implemented tax rebates on key projects of integrated circuit and excess VAT paid on some imported equipment since November 1, 2011, and exempted value-added tax on fresh vegetables, meat and egg products in circulation since 2012. Implementation of these structural tax cut policies correspondingly reduced revenue from value-added tax.

China raised the threshold for levying business tax since November 1, 2011; and a pilot program was launched in Shanghai to replace the business tax with VAT in certain service sectors, such as the transportation sector, starting from January 1, 2012, causing revenue from business tax to reduce correspondingly in both sectors. Moreover, business tax for entertainment applies two tax rates. Particularly, the tax rate for golf was adjusted from 20% to 10%, while that for entertainment programs were from 20% to 5%. Changes to the tax rate shall not be neglected.

From December 1, 2012 to December 31, 2015, the tax base for small and micro-sized companies with annual corporate income of no more than 60, 000 yuan as enterprises micro-and-small-sized companies. After the adjustment, their tax base will be cut by 50 percent while the tax rate remains 20 percent. As a result of the more loosened new policy for small and micro-sized companies implemented in 2012, the threshold of taxable income was raised from 30000 yuan to 60000, causing revenue from corporate income tax to reduce correspondingly.

Since September 1, 2011, the reform on individual income tax raised the threshold for individual income tax on wages and salaries and the adjustment of tax rates for income tax on wages and income of self-employed industrial and commercial households largely reduced tax burdens on low and medium wage earners, appropriately lowered tax burdens on income from production and operation of self-employed industrial and commercial households, thus leading to a sharp decline in revenue from both items.

In addition, approved by the State Council, to encourage financial institutions to provide financial supports for and boost the development of small and micro-sized firms, the stamp tax on loan contracts signed by financial institutions with small and micro-sized firms shall be exempted from November 1, 2011 to October 31, 2014, causing revenue from stamp tax to reduce correspondingly.

2.4 Treasury Bonds Issued in 2012

2.4.1 Overview of Treasury Bonds in 2012

Comparing the budgeted figures of 2012 released at the start of 2012 with final accounts of 2011, it can be seen that the growth rate of total central revenue was 9% in 2012, far behind the growth rate of total central expenditure at 13.7%. However, based on the budget deficit, the deficit of 2012 dropped sharply from that of 2011, because the 270 billion yuan from the central budget stabilization fund became revenue used by the central government. The growth rate of the balance of treasury bonds was 14.8%. By referring to data of recent years, its value remained at the middle level, and slightly dropped from the growth rate of 15.0% in 2011. Decline in the budget deficit as well as the balance of treasury bonds, on one side, was attributed to the "4 trillion" investment plan gradually digested after the financial crisis in 2008; and on the other, represents the prudent attitude of the central government toward the current economic situation, giving more attention to adjustment of the economic structure, leading the growth of treasure bonds issued back to normal.

By adopting the outstanding balance management of treasury bonds, with the approval of the National People's Congress, the outstanding balance of treasury bonds at the end of 2012 was limited to 8.270835 trillion yuan. As implementation of the 2012 budget is not released yet, the structure of outstanding treasury bonds is currently unknown. In reference to data in past years, domestic debt continued to account for above 99%.

Table 2. 5 Fiscal Revenue and Expenditure and Debt in 2011 and 2012

(Unit: 100 million yuan, %)

Item	Final account of 2011	Budgeted figure of 2012	Growth rate
Total central revenue	51306. 15	55920	9
Total central expenditure	56414. 15	64120	13. 7
Budget deficit	6500	5500	− 15. 4
outstanding balance of government bonds in the central budget	72044. 51	82708. 35	14. 8

Source: Report on the Implementation of Central and Local Budgets for 2011 and on Draft Central and Local Budgets for 2012 released by the Ministry of Finance.

2. 4. 2 Structure of outstanding treasury bonds in 2011

Analyzed by components of the outstanding balance of treasury bonds, among the actual outstanding balance of treasury bonds at the end of 2011, domestic debt was 7141. 1 billion yuan and external debt totaled 63. 4 billion yuan, respectively accounting for 99. 1% and 0. 9% of the total balance.

As regards the size and structure of sovereignty debt, the Chinese government totally borrowed 131. 044 billion dollars of external debt, a balance of 71. 579 billion dollars by the end of 2010. Of registered sovereignty debt, loans from international financial organizations, including the World Bank and Asian Development Bank, amounted to 58. 797 billion dollars, a balance of 33. 733 billion dollars by the end of the year; bilateral preferential loans from 26 state and regional financial institutions based in Japan, German, France and Kuwait were 59. 265 billion dollars, a balance of 32. 084 billion dollars; 30 batches of bonds totaling 12. 982 billion dollars were issued to overseas markets in Renminbi and foreign currencies, a balance of 5. 762 billion dollars.

Based on the balance of domestic debt by types of bonds, in 2010, the balance of savings treasury bonds totaled 886. 5 billion yuan, including certificate treasury bonds amounting to 586. 5 billion yuan and savings treasury bonds (electronic) totaling 300 billion yuan, accounting for 13. 1% of the outstanding balance of treasury bonds; and the balance of book-entry treasury bonds amounted to 5810. 4 billion yuan, including ordinary treasury bonds totaling 4260. 2 billion yuan and special treasury bonds amounting to 1550. 2 billion yuan, accounting for 86. 1% of the outstanding balance of treasury bonds.

By terms of outstanding treasury bonds, the average remaining term of outstanding treasury bonds at the end of 2010 was 8. 1 years (excluding that of external debts), 0. 4 years longer than that at the end of 2009. Among outstanding treasury bonds at the end of 2010, bonds with a term of 1 year or below accounted for 16%, that of 1 to 5 years (including 5 years) 27. 7%, that of 5 to 10 years (including 10 years) 26. 3% and that above 10 years 30%. [1]

2.4.3 Types of treasury bonds issued in 2012

(1) Tradable treasury bonds

Tradable treasury bonds issued in China are mainly book-entry treasury bonds, including discount bonds and coupon bonds. In 2012, China continued to use the subdivision method of book-entry treasury bonds adopted in past years, including book-entry discount bonds and book-entry coupon bonds numbered independently.

By December 2012, China issued 8 batches of book-entry discount bonds, totaling 120 billion yuan, and 21 batches of book-entry coupon bonds in 37 times (as the 4th, 5th, 9th, 10th, 15th and 16th batches were re-issued two times and the 3rd, 7th, 14th and 17th batches were re-issued one time), amounting to 1. 08328 trillion yuan.

In general, book-entry treasury bonds issued in 2012 had the following characteristics: the issuance of book-entry discount bonds continued to decline while that of book-entry coupon bonds remained stable; medium and long-term coupon bonds, such as the 4th, 5th, 9th, 10th, 15th and 16th batches, were re-issued two times, with a total accounting for 50. 51% of total treasury bonds issued. Re-issuance gradually took the place of new issuance to become a new mode of fund raising. The reason might be rooted in that: under the mode of annual balance management, the Ministry of Finance tended to issue

---

[1] As relevant data are still not released, we have to analyze the size and structure of China's external debts and the type and term structure of outstanding domestic debts on the basis of data at the end of 2010 published on the website of the Ministry of Finance.

long-term treasury bonds (which can alternatively increase the use of funds raised), reduce or not issue short-term treasury bonds with a maturity of less than 1 year.

(2) Non-tradable treasury bonds

China issues two types of non-tradable treasury bonds: one is certificate treasury bonds and the other savings treasury bonds. In 2012, China issued 3 batches of certificate treasury bonds amounting to 80 billion yuan and 14 batches of savings treasury bonds totaling 170 billion yuan (including the 5th, 6th, 7th and 8th batches that were stopped from issuing since the date the People's Bank of China adjusted the benchmark interest rate for deposits of the same term at financial institutions).

Compared with that in 2011, among non-tradable treasury bonds issued in 2012, issuance volume of certificate treasury bonds reduced sharply while that of savings treasury bonds remained stable. The volume of certificate treasury bonds reduced from 140 billion yuan in 2011 to 80 billion yuan, a drop of 43%; that of savings treasury bonds rose up from 160 billion yuan in 20110 to 170 billion yuan, a rise of 6.25%. The total volume of non-tradable treasury bonds declined from 300 billion yuan in 2011 to 250 billion yuan in 2012, down by 17%. This reflects the trend that tradable treasury bonds are increasingly favored by investors while non-tradable treasury bonds are in a relative slump.

(3) Summary on types of treasury bonds issued

First, treasury bonds maintained their original characteristics in terms of bond type. On one hand, tradable treasury bonds continued to dominate the market. Book-entry treasury bonds stood for 80.5% of total treasury bonds issued in 2011, and slightly increased to 81.2% in 2012. At the same time, book-entry coupon bonds had a growing proportion in book-entry treasury bonds. On the other hand, of non-tradable treasury bonds, savings treasury bonds exceeded certificate treasury bonds for the second consecutive year since its first issuance in 2006, reaching a proportion of 68% in 2012. The trend of savings treasury bonds issued in electronic forms exactly illustrates the development tendency of products currently issued in the financial market.

Second, the issuance frequency and volume of treasury bonds declined, but remained at a high level. As for the frequency, treasury bonds were issued 54 times in 2012, a little less than 65 times in 2011. In terms of volume, China issued a total of 1.33328 trillion yuan worth of treasury bonds in 2012, 25.4% lower than the total of 1.78819 trillion yuan in 2009. Decline of treasury bonds issued was in line with the prudent fiscal policy the Chinese government currently adopted. The "4 trillion yuan" investment plan initiated at the end of 2008 continued to be digested and the declined scale of treasury bonds effectively alleviated inflationary pressures.

2.4.4 Terms of treasury bonds issued in 2012

(1) Terms of book-entry treasury bonds

Usually, the government issued bonds with different terms and China was not an exception. Around the world, there is not a unified criterion to divide the terms of treasury bonds. Here, we define treasury bonds with a term less than 1 year as short-term treasury bonds, that having a term ranging from 1 year to less than 10 years as medium-term treasury bonds and those carrying a term of 10 years or more as long-term treasury bonds. Term structure of book-entry treasury bonds can be analyzed in aspects of short-term, medium-term and long-term as defined in the above.

In China, short-term book-entry treasury bonds carrying a maturity term less than 1 year are issued on a discount basis. In 2012, the Ministry of Finance issued 8 batches of book-entry discount bonds totaling 120 billion yuan in the treasury bond market. Terms of these bonds were below 1 year, namely, 91 days, 182 days and 273 days respectively. Of them, treasury bonds with a maturity term of 91 days were issued in 2 batches, totaling 30 billion yuan; 182 days in 3 batches, totaling 45 billion yuan and 273 days in 3 batches, 45 billion yuan.

Medium-term book-entry treasury bonds with different terms are issued at coupon interest paid annually. In 2012, the Ministry of Finance increased the issuance of medium-term book-entry treasury bonds to 21 batches with a volume totaling 612.97 billion yuan in terms of 1 year, 3 years, 5 years and 7 years. To be specific, in 2012, the Ministry of Finance issued 4 batches of 1-year book-entry bonds amounting to 108.95 billion yuan; 4 batches of 3-year bonds at a volume of 118.12 billion yuan; 4 batches of 5-year bonds worth 114.06 billion yuan; and 9 batches of 7-year bonds totaling 271.84 billion yuan.

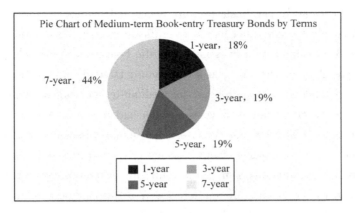

Figure 2. 4 Terms of Medium-term Book-entry Treasury Bonds

Long-term book-entry treasury bonds are also coupon-bearing bonds, but the interest will be paid semiannually instead of annually. Terms of long-term book-entry treasury bonds include 10 years, 20 years, 30 years and 50 years. In general, 8 batches of long-term book-entry treasury bonds were issued in 2012, totaling 470. 31 billion yuan, up 105% compared with 229. 08 billion yuan 2010. In 2012, the Ministry of Finance issued 10 batches of 10-year book-entry bonds, totaling 304. 31 billion yuan in volume, accounting for 64. 7% of all long-term treasury bonds issued that year, only 2 batches of 20-year book-entry bonds with a volume of 56 billion yuan, 2 batches of 30-year book-entry bonds with a volume of 56 billion yuan, and 2 batches of 50-year bonds worth of 54 billion yuan.

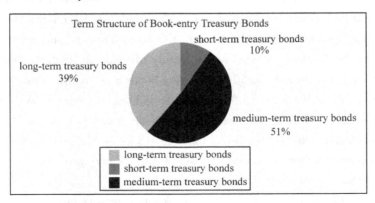

Figure 2. 5 Term Structure of Book-entry Treasury Bonds

(2) Terms of certificate treasury bonds and savings treasury bonds

It should be noted that terms of certificate treasury bonds returned to the original 3-year and 5-year ones instead of the 1-year and 3-year classifications in the past 3 years. Actually, as a type mainly targeting at attracting individual savings funds, it was appropriate for medium-term certificate treasury bonds to have terms of 3 years or 5 years, which had remained attractive for subscription. In 2009, the Chinese government reduced benchmark interest rates in order to address impacts of the financial crisis and further facilitate implementation of the stimulus plan. As a result, the coupon interest rates of certificate treasury bonds with different terms were correspondingly reduced, so that certificate treasury bonds with relatively longer terms were not attractive enough in the market. Under this situation, the original 3-year and 5-year certificate treasury bonds were respectively conversed to 1-year and 3-year ones since the second half of 2009.

Terms structure of savings treasury bonds. In 2010, China issued 14 batches of savings treasury bonds, including 7 batches of 3-year bonds and 7 batches of 5-year bonds. The 3-year savings treasury bonds issued in 2012 raised 166 billion yuan while the 5-year ones raised 74 billion yuan.

2.4.5 Interest rate of treasury bonds issued in 2012

Issued by the central government and guaranteed by the country's fiscal strengths and national credit, treasury bonds have the highest reputation, best safety and minimum risk in the bond market. According to the principle of risk-return trade-off in the market, interest rates of treasury bonds are often very low in the market interest rate system and can be referred to as the benchmark interest rate in the market. However, treasury bonds currently issued by the Chinese government are mainly divided into tradable book-entry bonds and non-tradable certificate treasury bonds and savings treasury bonds. Book-entry bonds are issued through public bidding, carrying market-oriented interest rates. But for non-tradable certificate treasury bonds and savings treasury bonds, the coupon rate at time of issuance is designed by the Ministry of Finance in reference to bank's interest rate for savings deposit having the same term.

(1) Changes to interest rates of book-entry treasury bonds

In 2012, China issued 8 batches of book-entry discount bonds, which in-

cluded 2 batches with a term of 91 days, totaling 30 billion yuan, 3 batches
with a term of 182 days, worth of 45 billion yuan and 3 batches with a term of
273 days, a volume of 45 billion yuan. The following table shows interest
rates of each batch of book-entry discount bonds issued.

Table 2.6 Book-entry Discount Bonds Issued in 2012

Batch	Volume (100 million yuan)	Issue price (yuan)	Term (days)	Interest rate (%)	Value date
1st	150	100.47	273 days	2.87	April 16
2nd	150	97.953	273 days	2.81	May 7
3rd	150	98.342	273 days	2.27	June 18
4th	150	98.899	182 days	2.26	July 16
5th	150	98.829	182 days	2.4	July 30
6th	150	98.799	182 days	2.47	August 6
7th	150	99.289	91 days	2.94	October 22
8th	150	99.242	91 days	3.13	November 5

Source: Calculated based on data released on the website of the Ministry of Finance as of December
18. The volume refers to the actual volume issued.

In general, changes to interest rates of book-entry discount bonds fea-
tured the shape of "V" in 2012, basically due to two reasons: on one hand,
due to effects of the tight monetary policy taken in the past two years, CPI inflation was obviously controlled so that the government implemented a loose
monetary policy, causing the interest rates of treasury bonds issued to go low;
on the other hand, affected by the carryover effect at the end of the year, inflation expectations were strengthened, causing the interest rate to climb up.
Based on specific types of treasury bonds, for issuance of 273-day and 182-
day book-entry discount bonds, the interest rate was on the decline. Certain-
ly, issuance at the year-end was affected by money supply in the market due
to special reasons. Throughout the year, the interest rate grew up largely.
Therefore, the interest rate of 2 batches of 92-day book-entry discount bonds
issued at the year-end climbed up slightly.

In 2012, China issued 37 batches of book-entry coupon bonds with 4
kinds of maturity terms. Similar to book-entry discount bonds, interest rates of

book-entry coupon bonds issued in 2012 were generally on the decline and moved up at the year-end. Based on different maturity terms, 1-year and 10-year treasury bonds were issued in 4 batches respectively, spanning throughout the year. Changes to these two bonds significantly reflected changes to interest rates all over the year. The interest rate of 1-year book-entry coupon bonds fell down from 2. 78% of the first batch (issued on January 12) to 2. 15% of the third batch (issued on June 14), and returned to 2. 94% of the last batch (on October 18); issues of 10-year book-entry coupon bonds were the most among all types issued in 2012 (including re-issuance). Its interest rate was 3. 51% of the first batch (February 23), 3. 36% of the second batch (May 24), 3. 39% of the third batch (August 23) and 3. 55% of the last batch (December 13). Based on interest rates of both types of bonds, the interest rate of 2012 was generally in line with the V curve, hitting the bottom in June and July.

(2) Changes to interest rates of certificate treasury bonds and savings treasury bonds

In 2012, China issued 3 batches of certificate treasury bonds, with 2 types of terms, namely, 3 years and 5 years. Based on the data, the last 2 batches had basically the same interest rate. In addition, both the last 2 batches were issued in the second half of 2012, one lasting from August 10 to 19, and the other from October 10 to 19, an interval of 2 months, which indicates that interest rates in the early of the second half of 2012 had small fluctuations.

Next is the interest rate of savings treasury bonds. Savings treasury bonds issued in 2012 also had 2 types of terms, namely, 3 years and 5 years. Coupon interest rates of savings treasury bonds in both terms were the same of certificate treasury bonds issued most recently. Considering that interests of savings treasury bonds were paid annually while that of certificate treasury bonds were paid at time of maturity together with the principal, the interest rate of certificate treasury bonds should be slightly higher than that of savings treasury bonds so as to make up for returns on re-investment of interests paid at time of maturity together with the principal.

2.4.6 Local government bonds issued in 2012

Based on the subject of bonds issued, government bonds are divided into central government bonds and local government bonds. The former is usually called treasury bonds, determined and issued by the central government, and its revenue was incorporated into the central budget, allocated by the central finance, with the central government to repay its principal and interest. Local government bonds are usually called local bonds, issued and repaid by local governments. In consideration of fiscal risks, China's budget law currently forbids local governments to issue government bonds.

However the policy started to loosen in 2009 when the central finance broke through the current budget law and issued 200 billion yuan of local government bonds on behalf of local governments to address the international financial crisis and help local government solve the problem of insufficient funds to support the "4 trillion yuan" investment plan. These local government bonds were incorporated into provincial budget management, therefore called local government bonds issued by the Ministry of Finance on behalf of local governments.

In October 2011, the Ministry of Finance released a notice on "Pilot Measures for Local Governments to Issue Bonds in 2011" in its official website. According to the notice, Zhejiang province, Guangdong province and the cities of Shanghai and Shenzhen were permitted by the State Council to issue bonds on their own.

However, the policy was tightened again in June 2012 when the 27th plenary meeting of the standing committee of 11th National People's Congress reiterated the provision of the current Budget Law, "Unless otherwise regulated by the law or the State Council, local governments should not issue local government bonds". In 2012, not only the pilot was not expanded to more provinces, but also local government bonds of 32 provinces and municipals were still issued by the Ministry of Finance. Closely watched government bonds issued by local governments themselves were totally postponed this year. That makes us wonder how far it is for local governments to issue bonds independently. At the same time, attention should be paid to the problem of local debt crisis. According to data released by the National Audit Office, the balance of local government debts in China has already exceeded 10 trillion yuan, with a debt ratio of above 150%, which is very high in terms of debt risks. As pointed out by Analysis and Forecast on China's Macroeconomy from 2011 to 2012 released by Renmin University of China: China's local governments entered the peak of debt repayment in 2011, and the ratio of debt repayment reached 17% in 2012. This may partly explains why the central government re-tightened the policy for local governments to issue government bonds independently since 2012. At the same time, terms of local government bonds turned to be more standard, namely, the medium to long term of 3 years and 5 years.

In 2012, the Ministry of Finance issued 10 batches of local government bonds and raised 241.1 billion yuan for 32 provinces and municipals, as detailed in the table below:

Table 2.6 Local Government Bonds Issued in 2012

Province/City	Batch	Volume (100 million yuan)	Interest rate (%)	Term (years)
Qingdao	1st	7	2.76	3
	2nd	8	3.07	5
Guangxi	1st	35	2.76	3
	2nd	36	3.07	5
Hunan	1st	20	2.76	3
	2nd	20	3.07	5
Chongqing	1st	31	2.76	3
	2nd	32	3.07	5
Shannxi	1st	42	2.76	3
	2nd	43	3.07	5
Xinjiang	1st	36	2.76	3
	2nd	36	3.07	5
Gansu	1st	35	2.76	3
	2nd	35	3.07	5
Beijing	3rd	34	2.75	3
	4th	34	3.02	5
Shanxi	3rd	33	2.75	3
	4th	32	3.02	5

Province/City	Batch	Volume (100 million yuan)	Interest rate (%)	Term (years)
Heilongjiang	3rd	41	2.75	3
	4th	41	3.02	5
Jiangsu	3rd	55	2.75	3
	4th	55	3.02	5
Fujian	3rd	30	2.75	3
	4th	30	3.02	5
Ningxia	3rd	16	2.75	3
	4th	17	3.02	5
Qinghai	3rd	30	2.75	3
	4th	30	3.02	5
Ningbo	5th	8	2.74	3
	6th	9	3.31	5
Anhui	5th	56	2.74	3
	6th	55	3.31	5
Hubei	5th	51	2.74	3
	6th	52	3.31	5
Sichuan	5th	67	2.74	3
	6th	68	3.31	5
Yunnan	5th	49	2.74	3
	6th	49	3.31	5
Tianjin	7th	15	2.98	3
	8th	16	3.38	5
Xiamen	7th	5	2.98	3
	8th	5	3.38	5
Jiangxi	7th	45	2.98	3
	8th	46	3.38	5

Province/City	Batch	Volume (100 million yuan)	Interest rate (%)	Term (years)
Shandong	7th	39	2.98	3
	8th	40	3.38	5
Henan	7th	55	2.98	3
	8th	56	3.38	5
Hunan	7th	57	2.98	3
	8th	58	3.38	5
Hebei	9th	46	3.47	3
	10th	46		5
Inner Mongolia	9th	42	3.47	3
	10th	43		5
Liaoning	9th	30	3.47	3
	10th	30		5
Dalian	9th	7	3.47	3
	10th	8		5
Jilin	9th	40	3.47	3
	10th	41		5
Tibet	9th	5	3.47	3
	10th	5		5
Guizhou	9th	36	3.47	3
	10th	37		5

Source: Calculated based on data released on the website of the Ministry of Finance as of December 18. The volume refers to the actual volume issued.

Interest rate of the 10th batch and the volume actually issued were not published.

2.5 Comments on Fiscal Revenue in 2012 and Outlook for 2013

Fiscal revenue completed in 2012 had the following features:

(1) Based on the total amount of fiscal revenue, national revenue amounted to 11. 7210 trillion yuan, a growth of 1. 3335 trillion yuan or 12.8% over last year, or 12.2 percentage points lower than that in the same period of 2011. Of this total, the growth of tax revenue was down by 10. 5 percentage points, mainly affected by slowed economic growth, declined enterprise profits, dropped price increases, especially reduced PPI, and intensified efforts of the structural tax cut policy.

(2) Based on the movement trend, fiscal revenue in the first three quarters of 2012 fell down gradually and rose up in the last quarter, showing a pattern of decline from high to low and rebounce in the last quarter. As for monthly growth, compared to the "first high and then low" trend of fiscal revenue in 2011, the growth of national revenue in 2012 showed an obviously opposite trend of "slip month by month and rebounce in later months" except for a sharp fall in April, and grew up substantially in later months.

(3) Based on the hierarchical structure of fiscal revenue, central government revenue totaled 5. 6133 trillion yuan, up 480. 5 billion yuan or 9. 4% over last year, accounting for 47. 9%; local government revenue reached 6. 1077 trillion yuan, up 850 billion yuan or 16.2% over last year, accounting for 52. 1%. The growth of central government revenue exceeded local governments revenue because: tax on imports, value-added tax, individual income tax, vehicle purchase tax, stamp tax on stock transaction that totally or mostly belong to the central government revenue registered low growth or fell down, particularly the increased tax rebates on exports from the central government in full deducting from revenue, which had significant impacts on the growth of central government revenue; while business tax, other local taxes and local non-tax revenue that mainly belong to local governments revenue grew up rapidly to boost the growth of local governments revenue.

(4) Based on composition of fiscal revenue, among the 11. 7210 trillion yuan of national revenue, tax revenue was 10. 0601 trillion yuan, accounting for 85.8%; while non-tax revenue stood at 1. 42405 trillion yuan, 14. 1%. Tax revenue grew up by 12. 1% year on year while non-tax revenue went up by 17. 5%, making remarkable contributions to overall revenue growth. Based on the hierarchical structure of non-tax revenue, non-tax revenue of the central government reached 284. 9 billion yuan, up 5. 7%; non-tax revenue of

local governments stood at 1.3760 trillion yuan, up 20.3%.

Main features of tax revenue growth in 2012 were: First, the growth of total tax revenue fell down drastically; second, by quarters, the growth rate of tax revenue showed a trend of "declining gradually from high to low" and going up slightly in Quarter 4; third, growth rates of major taxes dropped sharply.

(5) Analyzed by the direction of tax reform, the policy of structural tax cuts continued to be implemented with further increased efforts. Tax revenue from items involved, such as value-added tax, business tax, corporate income tax, individual income tax and customs duties, reduced accordingly, and mainly led to decline in central government revenue. As for the effects, the policy alleviated tax burdens on small and medium-sized enterprises, particularly small and micro-sized companies, boosted employment and entrepreneurship, and strengthened domestic drives for economic growth. The new Individual Income Tax Law implemented and exemption of value-added tax on vegetable whole sale and retail sale protected and improved people's livelihood; the pilot reform to replace business tax with value-added tax was steadily advanced, which improved the system of value-added tax and boosted adjustment and optimization of economic structure and the growth of the service industry; the pilot program to levy business tax on logistic enterprises based on the gap between profits and costs was expanded to greater coverage and tax incentives were formulated for urban land use tax on land used for commodity warehousing facilities of logistic enterprises, which promoted the healthy development of logistics; low tax rates on imports were temporarily implemented to encourage imports of advanced technology and equipment, and energy, resource and raw material.

The year of 2013 was the first year to fully implement the spirits of the 18th National Congress of the CPC and the key year to continue implementation of the 12th Five-year Plan. The central economic work conference held at the start of the year put forward clear requirements for further deepening the reform, expanding the opening-up policy, accelerating promotion of new-type industrialization, informationization, urbanization and agricultural modernization, and realizing strategic adjustment of the economic growth pattern, set up the keynote to boost steady, sustainable and healthy economic growth. At the same time, the conference also strengthened that China shall continue to implement a proactive fiscal policy and a prudent monetary policy in 2013. It can be predicted that as China accelerates promoting domestic transformation and expanding domestic demands, the overall "macro environment" for development shall gradually recover. These shall have positive impacts on social and economic development, and set a good foundation for revenue growth.

Though there are favorable factors, we should also be aware of the fact that the basis for economic recovery is not solid and that the gap between revenue and expenditure continues to exist, mainly manifested in such aspects: affected by the macroeconomy and other factors, fiscal revenue growth tends to slow down. Influenced by the global financial crisis and trade protectionism, some industrial enterprises shall meet increased difficulties, tax revenue paid by the sector of manufacturing that is the major tax source of value-added tax and corporate income tax shall continue to drop. Additionally, revenue of land finance will be further weakened. Except for the factor of economic tax cuts, affected by the policy of structural tax cuts, such as the policy of transforming business tax into value-added tax, the growth rate of tax revenue shall continue to reduce.

In general, opportunities and challenges shall co-exist in 2013. As the international economy continues to have a lot of uncertainties, domestic economic performance shall be confronted with various difficulties at the same time of becoming stable. In terms of the macroeconomy, it is predicted that in 2013, domestic economic growth shall rise up slightly, price increases shall remain basically the same as that of 2012, economic performance of enterprises shall find it difficult to make a change, and efforts on structural tax cuts shall be enhanced. Fiscal revenue shall no longer maintain a rapid growth above GDP growth as in the past several years. Instead, its growth rate may drop to around 8% - 10%, lower than that in 2012.

Meanwhile, the central finance shall be faced with more pressures of revenue and expenditure than local finance in 2013. On one hand, pressures of expenditure faced by the central finance shall remain unchanged in contrast to local finance. On the other hand, tax on imports, value-added tax, and income tax that totally or mostly belong to central revenue maintain a growth at a low speed, while revenue from newly added taxes created by the tax reform, such as resource tax and property tax, mainly belong to local finance. Non-tax revenue of local governments will remain a rapid growth.

References:

1. Xinhua. net: The Ministry of Finance: Above 250 Million Extra-budgetary Funds Incorporated under Supervision, May 18, 2012, http://finance. jrj. com. cn/2012/05/18200513185770. shtml

2. The website of the Ministry of Finance, Report on the Implementation of Central and Local Budgets for 2011 and on Draft Central and Local Budgets for 2012 (Summary), March 5, 2012.

3. The website of the Ministry of Finance, Structural Analysis of Tax Revenue Growth in 2012, January 2013.

4. The website of the Ministry of Finance, Fiscal Revenue and Expenditure in 2012, January 2013.

5. The website of the Ministry of Finance, Report on the Implementation of Central and Local Budgets for 2012 and on Draft Central and Local Budgets for 2013 (Summary), March 5, 2013.

6. The Ministry of Finance, http://mof. gov. cn

7. National Bureau of Statistics of China, http://www. stats. gov. cn/

8. CEInet database, http://db. cei. gov. cn/

3 China's Fiscal Expenditure in 2012

3.1 Review on Final Accounts of Fiscal Expenditure in 2011

As the Chinese government strengthened and improved macroeconomic control in 2011, the national economy was developed in the direction designed by the macroeconomic control and people's living standard was increasingly promoted, making the year a good start for the twelfth Five-year Plan period. Based on this, fiscal development and reform was deepened and advanced and the government budget was well implemented. Final accounts of government expenditure, expenditure from government-managed funds and expenditure from state-owned capital operations were as below.

3.1.1 Final accounts of government expenditure

In 2011, total national expenditure reached 10. 924779 trillion yuan, a growth of 21. 6% over 2010[1]. Adding the 289. 2 billion yuan used to replenish the central budget stabilization fund and the 173. 464 billion yuan of local government expenditure carried forward to 2012, total national expenditure came to 11. 387443 trillion yuan, which therefore exceeded total national revenue by 850 billion yuan.

3.1.1.1 Final accounts of central government expenditure

First, according to final accounts of central government expenditure in 2011, central government expenditure amounted to 5. 643532 trillion yuan, 103. 8% of the budgeted figure and an increase of 16. 8%. This consisted of

---

[1] Unless otherwise stated, growth in *Review on Fiscal Expenditure in* 2011 refers to the growth corresponding to the year of 2010.

1. 651411 trillion yuan of spending at the central level, up 3. 3%, and 3. 992121 trillion yuan in tax rebates and transfer payments to local governments, an increase of 23. 4%. Adding the 289. 2 billion yuan used to replenish the central budget stabilization fund, central government expenditure totaled 5. 923732 trillion yuan. Total expenditure exceeded total revenue, leaving a deficit of 650 billion yuan, 50 billion less than the budgeted figure at the central level.

Second, based on the structure of final accounts of central government expenditure (See Table 3. 1), final accounts of 6 expenditure items were below their budgeted figures, including spending on urban and rural community affairs, spending on financial regulation, spending on land and meteorological affairs and etc. Except for the above 6 items, final accounts of other expenditure items were completed or exceeded the budgeted figures set at the beginning of the year. In particular, final accounts of spending on education, spending on culture, sports and media, expenditure on transportation, spending on resource exploration, electricity and information, and spending on guaranteeing adequate housing exceeded their budgeted figures by more than 10%. It can be seen that spending on guaranteeing adequate housing was the highest in exceeding the budgeted figure, which reflects the great importance the central government attached to construction of low-income housing projects. In addition, tax rebates amounted to 503. 988 billion yuan, general transfer payments totaled 1. 831134 trillion yuan[1], and special transfer payments posted 1. 656999 trillion yuan.

Thirdly, based on growth rates of final accounts of central government expenditure (See Table 3. 1), the item having the highest growth rate of 59. 84% was spending on guaranteeing adequate housing. 6 items registered a growth rate between 20% and 40%, such as spending on education, spending on culture, sports and media, and spending on social security and employment; 8 items posted a growth rate between 10% and 20%, such as spending on general public services, expenditure on diplomacy and spending on nation-

---

① General transfer payment to local governments in Table 3. 1 does not include transfer payments on education, social security and employment, medical and health care. Adding these transfer payments, the total shall be equal to this value.

al defense. In addition, expenditures of other items had a growth of less than 10%. Particularly, growth rates of spending on urban and rural community affairs, spending on resource exploration, electricity and information, spending on commercial and service industry, spending on financial regulation, post-earthquake restoration and reconstruction, and other expenditures were even below zero.

Table 3.1 Central Government Expenditure in 2011

(Unit: 100 million yuan, %)

Item	Budgeted figure	Final account	Final account as % of the budgeted figure	Growth over last year	central government expenditure	% in expenditureg at the central level
1. general public services	1118.84	1190.31	106.4	19.88	903.01	75.86
2. diplomacy	316.65	307.75	97.2	14.81	306.83	99.70
3. national defense	5835.91	5835.97	100	12.61	5829.62	99.89
4. public security	1617.32	1695.47	104.8	14.91	1037.01	61.16
5. education	2963.57	3268.59	110.3	28.31	999.05	30.57
6. science and technology	1944.13	2034.06	104.6	17.69	1942.14	95.48
7. culture, sports and media	374.43	415.88	111.1	31.61	188.72	45.38
8. social security and employment	4414.34	4715.77	106.8	23.87	502.48	10.66
9. medical and health care	1727.58	1747.78	101.2	17.67	71.32	4.08
10. energy conservation and environmental protection	1591.85	1623.03	102	12.47	74.19	4.57
11. urban and rural community affairs	154.04	142.89	92.8	-12.13	11.62	8.13
12. agriculture, forestry and water conservancy	4588.83	4785.26	104.3	23.34	416.56	8.71
13. transportation	2866.91	3299.03	115.1	26.89	331.11	10.04
14. resource exploration, electricity and information	744.86	826.96	111	-0.10	464.12	56.12
15. commercial and service industry	706.14	737.66	104.5	-7.99	26.93	3.65
16. financial regulation	452.21	451.6	99.9	-10.12	413.94	91.66
17. post-earthquake restoration and reconstruction	–	21.55	–	-97.29		0.00

(**Continued**)

Item	Budgeted figure	Final account	Final account as % of the budgeted figure	Growth over last year	central government expenditure	% in expenditureg at the central level
18. Land and meteorological affairs	454.89	431.77	94.9	16.68	231.61	53.64
19. guaranteeing adequate housing	1292.66	1799.35	139.2	59.84	328.82	18.27
20. grain, edible oils, and other materials reserve affairs	1130.5	890.62	78.8	12.28	540.08	60.64
21. budget reserves	500	–	–	–	0	0.00
22. interest payment for national debts	1839.84	1819.96	98.9	20.62	1819.96	100.00
23. other expenditure	567.22	344.83	60.8	−8.58	74.99	21.75
24. tax rebates to local governments	5067.99	5039.88	99.4	0.93	–	–
25. general transfer payments to local governments	12089.29	13009.35	107.6	25.72	–	–
Total	54360	56435.32	103.8	16.77	16514.11	29.62

Notes: Data sourced from the website of the Ministry of Finance and obtained through simple calculation.

Finally, based on percentages of expenditure at the central level, there were 10 items in 2011, which accounted for above 50% of total expenditure on each of them, including spending on general public services, spending on diplomacy and spending on national defense. Percentages of expenditure at the central level represent the responsibilities of the central government, as detailed in Table 3.1.

3.1.1.2 Final accounts of local government expenditure

First, based on overall results in final accounts of local governments expenditure, local governments expenditure in 2011 reached 9.273368 trillion yuan, 111.5% of the budgeted figure and an increase of 25.5%. Adding the 173.464 billion yuan of expenditure carried forward to next year, total expenditure reached 9.446832 trillion yuan. Local governments expenditure exceeded local governments revenue by 200 billion yuan.

Second, based on the structure of final accounts of local governments expenditure (See Table 3.2), except for spending on energy conservation and environmental protection, spending on land and meteorological affairs and that on grain, edible oils and other materials reserve affairs, other expenditure items completed or exceeded the budgeted figures. Expenditure on post-earthquake restoration and reconstruction exceeded the budgeted figure by 818. 2%, the largest excess; followed by spending on guaranteeing adequate housing with an excess of 52.4%; expenditure on interest payment for national debts and that on financial regulation also exceeded the budgeted figures by 48.7% and 44.4% respectively; other items exceeded the budgeted figures by below 30%. It should be pointed out that the above expenditure items included expenditure arranged by tax rebates and transfer payments from the central government.

Table 3.2 Local Government Expenditures in 2011

(Unit: 100 million yuan, %)

Item	Budgeted figure	Final account	Final account as % of the budget	Growth rate
1. general public services	8888.9	10084.77	113.5	18.6
2. diplomacy	1.22	2.75	225.4	135.5
3. national defense	182	198.29	109	26.3
4. public security	5219.68	5267.26	100.9	13.5
5. education	13476.46	15498.28	115	31
6. science and technology	1788.2	1885.88	105.5	18.7
7. culture, sports and media	1525	1704.64	111.8	22.4
8. social security and employment	9887.92	10606.92	107.3	22.2
9. medical and health care	5296.5	6358.19	120	34.4
10. energy conservation and environmental protection	2736.66	2566.79	93.8	8.2
11. urban and rural community affairs	6595	7608.93	115.4	27.3
12. agriculture, forestry and water conservancy	8906	9520.99	106.9	23
13. transportation	5746.05	7166.69	124.7	79.2

(Continued)

Item	Budgeted figure	Final account	Final account as % of the budget	Growth rate
14. resource exploration, electricity and information	3239.82	3547.26	109.5	18.4
15. commercial and service industry	1353	1394.79	103.1	11.1
16. financial regulation	163	235.34	144.4	58.1
17. post-earthquake restoration and reconstruction	19	174.45	918.2	-84.1
18. Land and meteorological affairs	1305	1289.74	98.8	11.8
19. guaranteeing adequate housing	2292	3491.87	152.4	75.4
20. grain, edible oils and other materials reserve affairs	783.15	729.48	93.1	4.9
21. budget reserves	640	–	–	-0
22. interest payment for national debts	379.44	564.12	148.7	68.2
23. other expenditure	2746	2836.25	103.3	9
Total	83170	92733.68	111.5	25.5

Notes: Data sourced from the website of the Ministry of Finance.

Finally, based on growth rates of major expenditure items, spending on transportation had the largest growth of 79.2%, followed by spending on guaranteeing adequate housing with a growth rate of 75.4%. This clearly reflects policy intentions of local governments. Other expenditure items directly related to people's life, such as spending on education, medical and health care, social security and employment, and culture, also saw sharp growth. Their growth rates were all above 20%, respectively 31%, 34.4%, 22.2% and 22.4%.

3.1.2 Final accounts of expenditure from government-managed funds

In 2011, expenditure from government-managed funds totaled 3.994661 trillion yuan, 50.1% of the budgeted figure, up 17.7%. Adding the expenditure of 221.139 billion carried forward to next year, total expenditure from government-managed funds came to 4.2158 trillion yuan. In the below we shall illustrate final accounts of expenditure from central and local governments-managed funds.

3.1.2.1 Final accounts of expenditure from central government-managed funds

In 2011, expenditure from central government-managed funds totaled 310.348 billion yuan, 85.8% of the budgeted figure and an increase of 2.9%. This total consisted of two parts. The first was 215.686 billion yuan of spending at the central level, down 5.6%, which included 68.292 billion yuan on railroad construction fund; 7.355 billion yuan on port development; 19.125 billion yuan from lottery ticket proceeds, which was spent on social welfare, sports, education and other public service programs; and 10.526 billion yuan from the central government fund for repaying rural power grid loans. See Table 3.3 for details of central government expenditure from central government-managed funds.

Table 3.3 Final Accounts of Central Government Expenditure from Government-managed Funds in 2011 (Unit: 100 million yuan, %)

Item	Budgeted figure	Final account	Final account as % of the budgeted figure	Final account as % of that in previous year
Central government fund for repaying rural power grid loans	105.95	105.26	99.3	102.3
Railroad construction fund	682.92	682.92	100	117.3
Civil aviation infrastructure development fund	90.34	72.48	80.2	182.3
Civil airport administration and development fees	87.77	54.36	61.9	116.3
Port development fees	101.71	73.35	72.1	84.2
Tourism development fund	2.81	2.3	81.9	105.5
Cultural development fees	17.69	8.45	47.8	149.6
National film industry development fund	3.46	0.56	16.2	14.6

(**Continued**)

Item	Budgeted figure	Final account	Final account as % of the budgeted figure	Final account as % of that in previous year
Compensable payment for newly used land		1.72		135.4
Forest vegetation recovery fees	0.71	0.2	28.2	153.8
Central government water conservancy construction fund	71.23	12.44	17.5	164.6
South-north water diversion project fund	37.13	30.82	83	202.8
Fund for providing ongoing aid to residents relocated to build large and medium-sized reservoirs	0.47	0.49	104.3	108.9
Large and medium-sized reservoirs fund				
Three Gorges reservoirs fund	1.5	0.31	20.7	
Financial expenditure for central special debt management	682.87	682.87	100	100
Lottery proceeds	244.02	191.25	78.4	137.5
National Major water conservancy project fund	158.19	166.75	105.4	124.4
Port dues on vessels	39.16	37.34	95.4	105.6
Fees collected by CCPIT	0.54			
Yangtze river channel maintaining fees	15.15	13.6	89.8	
Fund for disposing spent fuel of nuclear power plant	36.89	2.25	6.1	
Revenue from selling off railway assets	4.13	16.5	399.5	5
Radio rate occupation fees		0.63		
Other government-management fund	0.29	0.01	3.4	100
Total	2384.93	2156.86	90.4	94.4

Notes: Data sourced from the website of the Ministry of Finance.

In addition, transfer payments from the central government to local governments amounted 94.662 billion yuan, up 29.2%. And a total of 82.221 billion yuan was carried forward to 2012 from central government-managed funds.

3.1.2.2 Final accounts of expenditure from local government-managed funds

In 2012, expenditure from local government-managed funds totaled 3.778975 trillion yuan, 156% of the budgeted figure, an increase of 18.4%. This included 3.105226 trillion yuan of spending from proceeds of the sale of state-owned land use rights, consisting of 1.435875 trillion yuan paid out as compensation for land expropriation, housing demolition, and resident relocation; 677.486 billion yuan for developing and improving farmland, strengthening rural infrastructure, and subsidizing farmers; and 556.488 billion yuan on urban development allocated in accordance with the provisions of the Law on Urban Real Estate Administration. A total of 30.312 billion yuan from lottery ticket proceeds was spent on social welfare, sports, education, and other public service programs; 75.765 billion yuan was used to support building urban infrastructure; and 40.774 billion yuan from local education surcharges was earmarked for education. See Table 3.4 for detailed expenditure from local government-managed funds.

Table 3.4 Final Accounts of Expenditure from Local Government-managed Funds (Unit: 100 million yuan, %)

Item	Budgeted figure	Final account	Final account as % of the budget	Final as % of that in previous year
Fund for repaying rural power grid loans	24.01	30.7	127.9	142.1
Shanxi sustainable coal development fund	160	162.22	101.4	101.6
Shanxi power base construction fund		0.33		8.9
Fujian railway construction surcharges		0.17		20.5

Item	Budgeted figure	Final account	Final account as % of the budget	Final as % of that in previous year
Civil airport administration and development fees	99.07	62.32	62.9	41.6
Hainan toll surcharges on vehicles passing high grade roads	11.1	13.25	119.4	152.5
Transferring charging right of government-financed roads	14.03	18.78	133.9	103.3
Port construction fees	36.65	40.55	110.6	113
Bulk cement special fund	10.73	8.46	78.8	117.2
New wall materials fund	50.06	36.63	73.2	136.9
Tourism development fund	5.76	4.57	79.3	108.6
Cultural development fees	58.2	59.9	102.9	133.8
Local education surcharges	274.13	407.74	148.7	219.3
Jiangsu local education fund	2.59	1.5	57.9	67.6
National film industry development special fund	6.36	1.63	25.6	301.9
New vegetable plots development fund	7.08	8.01	113.1	124.2
Compensable payment for newly used land	1262.83	879.45	69.6	134.1
Forestry cultivation fund	28.78	35.4	123	115.9
Forest vegetation recovery fees	55.64	80.01	143.8	140.6
Water conservancy construction fund	190.56	336.85	176.8	135.3
South-north water diversion project fund	2	3.77	188.5	2513.3
Shanxi water resource compensation fees		14.97		108.9
Employment security fund for the disabled	140.55	134.22	95.5	129.1

(**Continued**)

Item	Budgeted figure	Final account	Final account as % of the budget	Final as % of that in previous year
Government housing fund	108.23	133.92	123.7	132
Urban public utility surcharges	170.73	215.09	126	128.3
Proceeds from the sale of state-owned land use rights	18260.64	31052.26	170.1	116.6
State-owned land return fund	669.37	1052.31	157.2	119.9
Agricultural land development fund	146.73	186.42	127	125.4
Fund for providing ongoing aid to residents relocated to build large and medium-sized reservoirs	292.27	156.74	53.6	99.2
Large and medium-sized reservoirs fund	20.12	21.83	108.5	134.1
Three Gorges reservoirs fund	9.59	5.87	61.2	97.3
Lottery proceeds	351.4	303.12	86.3	102.1
Urban infrastructure supporting fees	446.67	757.65	169.6	158
Fund for providing ongoing aid to residents relocated to build small-sized reservoirs	8.15	10.98	134.7	181.5
National Major water conservancy project fund	107.18	59.4	55.4	2495.8
Tolls	1059.42	1191.47	112.5	145.5
Port dues on vessels	6.41	6.96	108.6	127.2
Fees collected by CCPIT		2.51		234.6
Radio rate occupation fees		11.16		
Other government-management fund	129.93	280.63	216	162.7
Total	24226.97	37789.75	156	119.3

Notes: The same as Table 3.3.

3.1.3 Final accounts of expenditure from state-owned capital operations

As limited by data availability, we just include final accounts of expenditures from the central government's state-owned capital operations. In 2011, expenditure from the central government's state-owned capital operations came to 76.953 billion yuan, 89.6% of the budgeted figure and an increase of 42%. The difference between the actual and budgeted amounts was mainly due to proceeds from the sale of state shares of enterprises being less than expected, which resulted in a corresponding reduction in expenditure. This figure included 49.166 billion yuan for restructuring the state-owned economy and industrial restructuring, 2.312 billion yuan in subsidies for reforming central government enterprises and making them profitable, 3.5 billion yuan for fostering major scientific and technological innovations, 3.5 billion yuan for major energy conservation and emissions reduction projects, 2.318 billion yuan for overseas investment, 955 million yuan for strengthening production safety, 8 billion yuan for enterprise mergers and reorganizations, 2.609 billion yuan for supporting emerging industries, and 4 billion yuan transferred to the public finance budgets and spent on social security, as shown in Table 3.5.

Table 3.5 Final Accounts of Central Government's State-owned Capital Operations (Unit: 100 million yuan, %)

Item	Budgeted figure	Final account	Final account as % of the budgeted figure	Final account as % of that in previous year
Central government enterprise mergers and reorganizations	80	80	100	
Fund for restructuring the state sector and industrial restructuring	495.5	491.66	99.2	273.9
Subsidies for reforming central government enterprises and making them profitable	30.5	23.12	75.8	19
Fund for fostering major scientific and technological innovations of central government enterprises	35	35	100	109.4

(**Continued**)

Item	Budgeted figure	Final account	Final account as % of the budgeted figure	Final account as % of that in previous year
Major energy conservation and e-missions reduction projects of central government enterprises	35	35	100	116.7
Overseas investment of central government enterprises	30	23.18	77.3	103.4
Strengthening production safety of central government enterprises	10	9.55	95.5	
Social security of central government enterprises	5	5.42	108.4	115.3
Budget for state-owned capital operations to replenish the national social security fund	50	0.51	1	0.4
Fund for supporting emerging industries	45	26.09	58	
Fund transferred to the public finance budget and spent on social security	40	40	100	400
Reserves	2.56			
Expenditure of central government state-owned capital operations	858.56	769.53	89.6	142
Expenditure carried forward to next year		31.07		87.3

Notes: The same as Table 3.3.

3.2 Budgets for fiscal expenditure in 2012

At the fifth session of the eleventh National People's Congress on March 5, 2012, the Ministry of Finance issued the Report on the Implementation of

Central and Local Budgets for 2011 and on Draft Central and Local Budgets for 2012, making explanations to the 2012 budgets for public finance, government-managed funds and state-owned capital operations. In the following, we shall make a brief analysis of its major expenditure targets.

3.2.1 Budgets for the 2012 fiscal expenditure

In 2012, national fiscal expenditure shall amount to 12.43 trillion yuan, up 14.1%. Of this amount, central government expenditure should total 6.412 trillion yuan, an increase of 13.7%; local government expenditure will reach 10.5281 trillion yuan, a growth of 13.9%. Among central government expenditure, 1.8519 trillion yuan will be incurred at the central level, up 12.1%; 4.5101 trillion yuan to be paid out as tax rebates and transfer payments to local governments, up 13%; and 50 billion yuan to be used as reserve funds in the central budget, the same as the budgeted figure for 2011. Expenditure was to exceed revenue by 800 billion yuan in the central budget, 50 billion yuan less than the previous year, causing its proportions in GDP reduced to about 1.5% and leaving a deficit of 550 billion yuan, down by 100 billion from final accounts of 2011.

3.2.1.1 Budgets for central government expenditure

Table 3.6 presents the budgets for major items of central government expenditure in 2012. It can be known from Table 3.6 that the budgeted figure of other expenditure in 2012 had the largest growth of 58.1% over the figure implemented in the previous year; spending on guaranteeing adequate housing, spending on social security and employment, spending on culture, sports and media, spending on medical and health care and spending on education ranked respectively No.2 to No. 5 in growth, up by above 15%, which reflects priorities of central government expenditure in 2012. Except for spending on urban and rural community affairs and spending on commercial and service industry that were down 38.9% and 35.6% respectively, all the other items had different growths compared to figures implemented last year.

Table 3.6 Budgets for Central Government Expenditure in 2012

(Unit: 100 million yuan, %)

Item	Budgeted figure in 2012	Growth of budgeted figure over that implemented last year	Ranking by growth
1. general public services	1230.61	3.4	18
2. diplomacy	342.31	11.2	11
3. national defense	6503.11	11.4	10
4. public security	1826.64	7.7	16
5. education	3781.32	16.4	5
6. science and technology	2285.46	12.4	9
7. culture, sports and media	493.84	18.7	4
8. social security and employment	5750.73	21.9	3
9. medical and health care	2035.05	16.4	5
10. energy conservation and environmental protection	1769.10	9.0	14
11. urban and rural community affairs	87.25	-38.9	21
12. agriculture, forestry and water conservancy affairs	5491.45	14.8	8
13. transportation	3565.93	8.1	15
14. resource exploration, electricity and information affairs	877.26	6.1	17
15. commercial and service industry affairs	474.72	-35.6	20
16. financial regulation affairs	452.55	0.2	19
17. post-earthquake restoration and reconstruction	-	-	-
18. Land and meteorological affairs	475.99	10.2	12
19. guaranteeing adequate housing	2117.55	23.1	2
20. grain, edible oils and other materials reserve affairs	974.19	9.4	13
21. interest payment for national debts	2093.68	15.0	7

Item	Budgeted figure in 2012	Growth of budgeted figure over that implemented last year	Ranking by growth
22. other expenditure	593.89	58.1	1
23. tax rebates to local governments	5188.55	2.2	–
24. general transfer payments to local governments	15208.82	16.8	–
Central government expenditure and subsidies to local governments	63620.00	12.8	–
reserves in the central budget	500.00	–	–
central government expenditure	64120.00	13.7	–

Notes: Data sourced from the website of the Ministry of Finance.

Second, based on the budgets for central government expenditure (as shown in Table 3.7), except for spending on energy conservation and environmental protection, spending on urban and rural community affairs, spending on resource exploration, electricity and information, spending on commercial and service industry, and spending on land and meteorological affairs that had negative growth, budgeted figures of all the remaining items were increased from figures implemented last year. Similar to the budgets for central government expenditure, the item that had the largest growth was other expenditure with a growth up to 444.6%. In addition, transportation, and medical and health care also grew up rapidly. The table also lists proportions of central government spending, which reveals that expenditure on diplomacy and that on interest payment for national debts were totally accounted by the central government, in addition to 99.63% of spending on national defense and 97.77% of spending on science and technology. What's more, above 50% of spending on general public services, spending on public security, spending on resource exploration, electricity and information, spending on financial regulation, expenditure on grain, edible oils, and other materials reserve affairs and other expenditure were paid by the central government.

Table 3.7 Budgets for spending at the central level

(Unit: 100 million yuan, %)

Item	Budgeted figure in 2012	Budget growth over final account of previous year	Percentage of expediture at the central level
1. general public services	946.84	4.9	76.94
2. diplomacy	342.31	11.6	100.00
3. national defense	6479.2	11.1	99.63
4. public security	1142.89	10.2	62.57
5. education	1028.87	3	27.21
6. science and technology	2234.4	15	97.77
7. culture, sports and media	207.33	9.9	41.98
8. social security and employment	570.63	13.6	9.92
9. medical and health care	83.31	16.8	4.09
10. energy conservation and environmental protection	63.44	-14.5	3.59
11. urban and rural community affairs	6.95	-40.2	7.97
12. agriculture, forestry and water conservancy affairs	427.44	2.6	7.78
13. transportation	434.65	31.3	12.19
14. resource exploration, electricity and information affairs	450.6	-2.9	51.36
15. commercial and service industry affairs	23.14	-14.1	4.87
16. financial regulation affairs	397.35	4	87.80
17. post-earthquake restoration and reconstruction	–	–	–
18. Land and meteorological affairs	193.54	-16.5	40.66
19. guaranteeing adequate housing	374.4	13.9	17.68
20. grain, edible oils, and other materials reserve affairs	609.57	12.9	62.57

(**Continued**)

Item	Budgeted figure in 2012	Budget growth over final account of previous year	Percentage of expediture at the central level
21. interest payment for national debts	2093.68	15	100.00
22. other expenditure	408.46	444.6	68.78
central government spending	18519	12.1	—

Notes: Data taken from the website of the Ministry of Finance and simply calculated.

Last, we shall make a brief review on central government tax rebates and transfer payments to local governments. In 2012, central government tax rebates and transfer payments to local governments totaled 4.5101 trillion yuan, an increase of 13%. This figure included 518.855 billion yuan in tax rebates, up 2.2%, 2.252619 trillion yuan in general transfer payments, a growth of 23.1%, and 1.738626 trillion yuan in special transfer payments, an increase of 5.2%. Of general transfer payments, balanced transfer payments totaled 858.365 billion yuan, only standing for 21.5% of total transfer payments. The percentage of balanced transfer payments was too small that it was not good for narrowing the remarkable financial gap between regions. Additionally, transfer payments was 168.032 billion yuan for compulsory education, 377.438 billion yuan for basic pension benefits and subsistence allowances, 106.348 billion yuan for the new rural cooperative medical care system, 25.309 billion yuan for awards and subsidies to village-level public works projects, and 78.4 billion yuan for reforming taxes and fees on refined petroleum products.

3.2.1.2 Budgets for local governments expenditure

In 2012, the budgets for local governments expenditure totaled 10.52809 trillion yuan, and growths of major expenditure items arranged are shown in Table 3.8. From the table we can see that spending on education had the largest growth of 18.4%, which reflects efforts made by the Chinese government to realize the target of spending on education accounting for 4% of GDP; the item that followed was spending on social security and employment, a growth of 16.2%; spending on culture, sports and media and spending on medical and health care also received a high a growth of above 15% respectively. Furthermore, except for post-earthquake restoration and reconstruction, all the remaining items had a growth of 5% -15%.

Table 3.8 Budget for Local Government Expenditure in 2012

(Unit: 100 million yuan, %)

Item	Budgeted figure of 2012	Budget growth over final account of previous year	Ranking by growth	Percentage	Ranking by percentage
1. general public services	10720	5.0	21	10.182	4
2. diplomacy	2.97	7.2	20	0.003	22
3. national defense	223.54	13.4	8	0.212	20
4. public security	5874.74	11.8	12	5.580	8
5. education	17900.24	18.4	1	17.002	1
6. science and technology	2110.3	13.2	9	2.004	13
7. culture, sports and media	1971.5	15.9	3	1.873	14
8. social security and employment	12367.29	16.2	2	11.747	2
9. medical and health care	7264.6	15.4	4	6.900	7
10. energy conservation and environmental protection	2901.92	14.1	7	2.756	12
11. urban and rural community affairs	8586.05	12.4	11	8.155	5
12. agriculture, forestry and water conservancy affairs	10816.77	14.2	6	10.274	3
13. transportation	7789.9	9.1	17	7.399	6
14. resource exploration, electricity and information	3872.6	9.1	17	3.678	10
15. commercial and service industry affairs	1507.2	8.8	19	1.432	15
16. financial regulation affairs	258.5	10.2	15	0.246	19
17. post-earthquake restoration and reconstruction	50	−71.5	22	0.047	21

Item	Budgeted figure of 2012	Budget growth over final account of previous year	Ranking by growth	Percentage	Ranking by percentage
18. Land and meteorological affairs	1423.4	11.4	13	1.352	16
19. guaranteeing adequate housing	4024	15.2	5	3.822	9
20. grain, edible oils, and other materials reserve affairs	808	11.1	14	0.767	17
21. interest payment for national debts	640	12.6	10	0.608	18
22. other expenditure	3217.38	10.2	15	3.056	11
23. budget reserves	950	–	–	–	–
Local governments expenditure	105280.9	13.9	–	100	–

Notes: Data obtained by deducting budgets for central government expenditure from budgets for national expenditure.

Table 3.8 also provides percentages of all the spending, which reflects responsibilities of local governments for spending on different affairs. It can be known from the table that spending on education remained the item with the largest percentage in local budgets, totaling 1.790024 trillion yuan and accounting for a percentage of 17.002% ; items that followed were spending on social security and employment totaling 1.236729 trillion yuan, a percentage of 11.747% , spending on agriculture, forestry and water conservancy affairs, 1.081678 trillion yuan and 10.274% , spending on general public services, 1.0720 trillion yuan and 10.182% . The item that accounted for the lowest percentage was spending on diplomacy, totaling 297 million yuan, only a percentage of 0.003% . All the remaining items accounted for a percentage between 0.003%-10% respectively. Expenditure on the above items included expenditure arranged by local governments from central government tax rebates and transfer payments.

3.2.2 Budgets for expenditure from government-managed funds

In 2012, national budgets for expenditure from government-managed funds totaled 3.561407 trillion yuan, down 10.2%. Of this figure, budgets arranged for expenditure from central and local governments-managed funds are respectively as below.

3.2.2.1 Budgets for expenditure from central government-managed funds

In 2012, expenditure from central government-managed funds will be 380.766 billion yuan, up 22.7% (as shown in Table 3.9). Based on growth rates of different items, expenditure from fund for disposing spent fuel of nuclear power plant has the greatest growth of up to 2103.1%, mainly caused by the small base of the previous year; followed are Three Gorges reservoirs fund, up 419.8%, Radio Rate Occupation Fees, up 289.6% and forestry cultivation fund, up 287.7%. Except for railway construction fund, compensable payment for newly used land, south-north water diversion project fund and Yangtze River channel maintaining revenue, all the remaining items receives different growths. In addition, based on percentages of these expenditure items, expenditure from financial revenue from central special debt management totals 68.287 billion yuan, standing for the largest percentage of 17.93%; items that followed are respectively expenditure from railway construction fund, totaling 68.04 billion yuan and accounting for 17.87%, lottery proceeds, 45.435 billion yuan and 11.93%, and compensable payment for newly used land, 38.631 billion yuan and 10.15%, while all the remaining items account for below 10% respectively.

Table 3.9 Budget Accounts of Central Government-managed Funds in 2012

(Unit: 100 million yuan, %)

Item	Budgeted figure of 2012	Budgeted figure as percentage of final accounts of previous year	Percentage
1. Rural Power Grid Loans Repaying Fund	109.68	104.2	2.88
2. Railway Construction Fund	680.4	99.6	17.87
3. Civil Aviation Airport Infrastructure Fund	79.35	109.5	2.08

Item	Budgeted figure of 2012	Budgeted figure as percentage of final accounts of previous year	Percentage
4. Civil Aviation Airport Administration and Development Fees	192.01	128.8	5.04
5. Port Construction Fees	127.45	110.8	3.35
6. Tourism Development Fund	8.66	123.7	0.23
7. Cultural Development Fees	21.57	206.2	0.57
8. National Film Industry Development Fund	11.55	250.5	0.30
9. Compensable Payment for Newly Used Land	386.31	84.5	10.15
10. Forestry Cultivation Fund	4.2	287.7	0.11
11. Water Conservancy Construction Fund	61.34	116.7	1.61
12. South-North Water Diversion Project Fund	26.95	87.4	0.71
13. Fund for Providing Ongoing Aid to Residents Relocated to Build Large and Medium-sized Reserviors	360.96	194.2	9.48
14. Large and Medium-sized Reservoirs Fund	4.38	115.3	0.12
15. Three Gorges Reservoirs Fund	13.56	419.8	0.36
16. Financial Revenue From Central Special Debt Management	682.87	100	17.93
17. Lottery Proceeds	454.35	159.6	11.93
18. National Major Water Conservancy Project Fund	334.38	200.5	8.78
19. Port dues on Vessels	49.49	132.5	1.30
20. Fees Collected by CCPIT	1.93	–	0.05
21. Yangtze River Channel Maintaining Revenue	2.54	18.7	0.07
22. Fund for Disposing Spent Fuel of Nuclear Power Plant	49.57	2203.1	1.30

(**Continued**)

Item	Budgeted figure of 2012	Budgeted figure as percentage of final accounts of previous year	Percentage
23. Revenue From Selling off Railway Assets	20. 13	122	0. 53
24. Revenue from Assets Liquidation of Electric Power Reform	60. 24	–	1. 58
25. Radio Rate Occupation Fees	45. 27	289. 6	1. 19
26. Waste Electrical and Electronic Products Processing Fund	15		0. 39
27. Other Government-management Fund	3. 52	166. 8	0. 09
Expenditure from central government-managed funds	3807. 66	122. 7	–

Notes: Data obtained through calculation after taken from the website of the Ministry of Finance.

3. 2. 2. 2 Budgets for expenditure from local governments-managed funds

In 2012, expenditure from local governments-managed funds will reach 3. 311674 trillion yuan, down 11. 7%. This total includes 2. 824105 trillion yuan from proceeds of the sale of state-owned land use rights, of which 1. 941571 trillion yuan will be spent on compensation for land expropriation, housing demolition, and resident relocation; 153. 492 billion yuan on developing and improving agricultural land, building rural infrastructure, and subsidizing farmers; 30. 594 billion yuan on education; 29. 797 billion yuan on building irrigation and water conservancy facilities; 62. 489 billion yuan on low-income housing projects; and 606. 162 billion yuan on urban construction. Expenditure from local government-managed funds also includes 31. 249 billion yuan from lottery ticket proceeds used to finance social welfare, sports, education, and other public welfare programs; 63. 744 billion yuan from supporting urban infrastructure construction fees; and 66. 599 billion yuan of education spending from local education surcharges.

3. 2. 3 Budgets for expenditure from state-owned capital operations

In 2012, total expenditure on state capital operations will reach 127. 756 billion yuan. Budgets for expenditure on the central government's and local governments' state capital operations are briefly illustrated as below.

3.2.3.1 Budgets for expenditure from state capital operations of the central government

In 2012, expenditure on state-owned capital operations of the central government will be 87.507 billion yuan, up 13.7%. Breaking it down, 8 billion yuan will be used for mergers and reorganizations of central government enterprises, 13.3 billion yuan for restructuring the state-owned sector and industrial restructuring, 11 billion yuan to foster major scientific and technological innovations, 8 billion yuan for energy conservation and emissions reductions, 8 billion yuan to support enterprises in "going global," 22.5 billion yuan to subsidize the reform of enterprises, 4.5 billion yuan to develop emerging industries, 2.01 billion yuan from the sale of state-owned shares of enterprises to replenish the national social security fund, 5.197 billion yuan for other expenditures related to SOE reforms and development, and 5 billion yuan to be transferred to the public finance budget and used for social security and other areas related to ensuring people's living standards.

3.2.3.2 Budgets for expenditure from local governments' state-owned capital operations

In 2012, expenditure on local governments' state-owned capital operations will amount to 40.249 billion yuan. Included in this sum is 3.046 billion yuan for mergers and reorganizations of enterprises, 16.698 billion yuan for restructuring the state-owned sector and industrial restructuring, 2.811 billion yuan for spurring scientific and technological innovations and industrialization, 1.679 billion yuan for energy conservation and emissions reductions, 7.02 billion yuan for subsidizing the reform of enterprises, and 4.91 billion yuan for other expenditures.

3.3 Scale of government expenditure in 2012

3.3.1 Implementation of fiscal budgets

For implementation of public finance budgets (as shown in Table 3.10), national expenditure in 2012 totaled 12.5712 trillion yuan, 141.2 billion yuan above the budgeted figure. To break down, central government expenditure amounted to 6.4148 trillion yuan, 2.8 billion yuan above the budgeted figure[1];

---

[1] Due to reduced budget reserves, the growth of central government expenditure was less than the sume of the growth of central government spending and the growth of central government tax rebates and transfer payments to local governments.

this consists of 1.8765 trillion yuan of central government expenditure, an increase of 60.6 billion yuan; and 4.5383 trillion yuan in tax rebates and transfer payments to local governments, a growth of 28.2 billion yuan. Local governments expenditure from local governments revenue, central government tax rebates and transfer payments totaled 10.6947 trillion yuan, a growth of 166.6 billion yuan.

In addition, based on the annual growth, national government expenditure in 2012 was 1.6464 trillion yuan above that of last year, up 15.1%. Central government expenditure was 768.468 billion yuan higher than the previous year, up 13.6%; of this total, central government expenditure was 225.1 billion yuan higher than last year, up 13.6%; tax rebates and transfer payments to local governments increased by 546.2 billion yuan, up 13.7%. local governments expenditure increased by 1.4214 trillion yuan, up 15.3%. Both the absolute amount and the growth rate in 2012 rose up sharply from 2011, mainly because China continued to implement an expansionary fiscal policy in 2012.

Table 3.10 Government Expenditure in 2012

(Unit: 100 million yuan, %)

Category		Budgeted Figure		Budget implemented	
		Amount	Growth rate	Amount	Growth rate
National government expenditure	Total amount	124300	14.1	125712	15.1
	National deficit	8000	−5.9	—	—
central government expenditure	Total amount	64120	13.7	64148	13.6
	Central government spending	18159	12.1	18765	13.6
	Tax rebates to local governments	45101	13	45383	13.7
	Central deficit	5500	−21.4	—	—
Local government expenditure	Total amount	105281	13.9	106947	15.3
	Local deficit	2500	25	—	—

Notes: Data obtained through simple calculation after taken from the website of the Ministry of Finance. "—" indicates that relative data are unavailable.

3.3.2 Analysis on relationship between government expenditure and revenue

As shown in Table 3.11, the growth rate of government expenditure was higher than that of government revenue throughout the year, mainly because: on one hand, management for implementation of expenditure budgets was further enhanced, and key expenditures on people's livelihood were practically guaranteed, thus causing expenditure growth to rise up substantially; on the other hand, affected by slowdown of the economic growth, decline in price hikes, drop of enterprise profits and implementation of structural tax reduction, tax revenue fell down sharply in growth. Based on the gap between government expenditure and revenue, national expenditure in 2012 reached 12.5712 trillion yuan, up 15.1%; government revenue of the same period reached 11.7210 trillion yuan, up 12.8%. By the growth rate, except for May, October, November and December, expenditure growths in other months were higher than revenue growths. Expenditure growth rate in Quarter 4 of 2012 was low because the base in the same period of 2011 was high. As government expenditure grew faster than revenue, the amount of government expenditure exceeded that of revenue. In 2012, total amount of government expenditure was 850.2 billion yuan above revenue.

Table 3.11 Monthly Government Expenditure and Revenue in 2012

(Unit: 100 million yuan, %)

Month	Government Expenditure		Government Revenue		Gap between expenditure and revenue
	Amount	Year-on-year Growth Rate	Amount	Year-on-year Growth Rate	
1-2	13924.14	32.8	20918.28	13.1	-6994.14
3	10193.91	34.7	9057.97	18.7	1135.94
4	7885	8	10774	6.9	-2889
5	9165	10.8	12005	13.1	-2840
6	12724	17.7	11040	9.8	1684
7	9528	37.1	10672	8.2	-1144
8	9020	11.7	7863	4.2	1157
9	11679	16.6	8258	11.9	3421

(**Continued**)

Month	Government Expenditure		Government Revenue		Gap between expenditure and revenue
	Amount	Year-on-year Growth Rate	Amount	Year-on-year Growth Rate	
10	8617	6.7	10444	13.7	- 1827
11	12160	6.7	7871	21.9	4289
12	20815.95	2.7	8306.75	26.6	12509.2
Total	125712	15.1	117210	12.8	8502

Notes: Data of the gap between government expenditure and revenue were obtained by deducting government revenue from government expenditure of the current month. Source: the website of the Ministry of Finance.

In addition, based on the relationship between growth rates of government expenditure and revenue in past years (as shown in Figure 3.1), except for 2000 and 2002, growth rates of government expenditure before 2007 were all below that of government revenue. However, as the growth rate of government revenue declined dramatically in 2008 and 2009, far below that of government expenditure, mainly because: on one hand, as the Chinese economy has been faced with severe global economic situations since the outbreak of the financial crisis in 2008, the growth rate of government revenue declined dramatically from previous years and hit the bottom of the past 10 years in 2009; on the other, as China implemented a proactive fiscal policy to address this severe economic situation, fiscal expenditure grew up substantially. Fiscal revenue went up sharply in 2010 and 2011, causing its growth rate exceeding the growth rate of fiscal expenditure; in 2012, the growth rate of fiscal revenue declined dramatically to only 12.8%, lower than the growth rate of fiscal expenditure. The growth rate of fiscal expenditure remained high mainly because implementation and management of expenditures in the budget was further intensified, and the growth rates of expenditure on people's livelihood, including education, medical and health care, and housing guarantees were high. The reasons why fiscal revenue reduced sharply in growth include: First, the economic growth slowed down and enterprise benefits slipped. In the first three quarters of 2012, GDP calculated at comparable prices went up by 7.7% (up 10% if calculated at current prices), 1.7 percentage points lower than that in the same period of last year; industrial added values by enterprises of designated size rose up by 10% (9.2% in September) based on comparable prices, down by 4.2 percentage points comparing that in the same period of last year, investment in fixed assets went up by 20.5%, or 4.4 percentage points lower year on year; retail sales of consumer goods grew up by 14.1%, or 2.9 percentage points lower; general trade import was up 3.6% (down 5.3% in September), or 29.7 percentage points lower; sales of commercial buildings went up by 2.7%, or 20.5 percentage points lower. Profits made by industrial enterprises of designated size in the first 8 months was down 3.1% (6.2% in August) or 31.3 percentage points lower. Accordingly, growths of tax items, including value-added tax, business tax, tax on imports and corporate income tax, declined sharply. Second, price increase fell down. In the first three quarters, CPI went up by 2.8% (1.9% in September), 2.9 percentage points lower than that in the same period of last year. Particularly, PPI was down 1.5% (3.6% in September), or 8.5 percentage points lower. Revenue growth from turnover taxes calculated at current prices dropped correspondingly. Third, efforts on structural tax cuts were huge. In 2012, China continued to implement structural tax cut policies to regulate income distribution, support the development of small and micro-sized companies, adjust the industrial structure, expand imports and stabilize prices, causing tax revenue from individual income tax, corporate income tax, value-added tax, business tax, customs duties to reduce relatively.

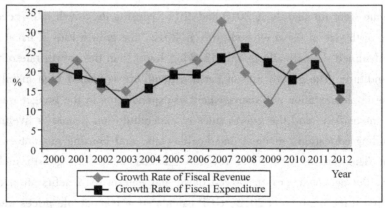

Figure 3.1 Growth Rates of Government Revenue and Expenditure in 2000-2012

3. 3. 3 Analysis on relationship between government expenditure and GDP

Table 3.12 reflects China's government expenditure, GDP growth rates and percentages of government expenditure in GDP in 2000-2012. It can be known from the table that: First, the growth rate of national government expenditure is affected by the economic growth. When the economic growth slows down, the growth rate of fiscal expenditure shall reduce correspondingly, though such reduction may be lagged for 1 or 2 periods. However, its reduction is far below that of GDP. By contrast, when GDP growth rises up, the growth rate of fiscal expenditure shall go up immediately. Second, except for in 2003 and 2004, China's national government expenditure grew up at a speed higher than GDP growth, mainly because: when the economic growth slows down, the government usually tends to implement an expansionary policy to stimulate economic growth. Therefore, when the economic growth slows down, fiscal expenditure grows up rapidly; when the economic growth is improved, due to fiscal rigidity, the growth rate of fiscal expenditure may not decline sharply even if it drops. At the same time, due to the ratchet effect, when the economy grows rapidly, it is impossible for fiscal expenditure to drop sharply, so the growth rates of government expenditure exceeded that of GDP in most years. Third, the ratio of government expenditure in GDP constantly rose up, basically in a trend of increase year by year. From 2000 to 2012, this ratio climbed up from 16% to 24.2%, only dropped slightly in 2003 and 2004, mainly caused by the growth rates of fiscal expenditure lower than GDP growth rates.

Table 3. 12 Relationship between Government Expenditure and GDP in 2000-2012 (Unit: %)

Year	Growth Rate		Percentage of government expenditure in GDP
	Government expenditure	GDP	
2000	20.5	9.1	16.0
2001	19.0	10.5	17.2
2002	16.7	9.7	18.3

Year	Growth Rate		Percentage of government expenditure in GDP
	Government expenditure	GDP	
2003	11. 8	12. 9	18. 1
2004	15. 6	17. 7	17. 8
2005	19. 1	15. 7	18. 3
2006	19. 1	17. 0	18. 6
2007	23. 2	22. 9	18. 7
2008	25. 7	18. 1	19. 9
2009	21. 9	8. 6	22. 3
2010	17. 8	17. 7	22. 4
2011	21. 6	17. 9	23. 1
2012	15. 1	7. 8	24. 2

Notes: Data obtained through calculation after taken from the website of the Ministry of Finance and China Statistics Yearbook.

3. 4 Structure of government expenditure in 2012

3. 4. 1 Structure of government expenditure by months

As shown in Table 3. 13, national government expenditure implemented in 2012 totaled 12. 5712 trillion yuan in 2012, a growth of 1. 6464 trillion yuan over 2011, or up 15. 1%. of this total, government expenditure in Quarter 1, 2, 3 and 4 were respectively 2. 411805, 2. 9774, 3. 0227 and 4. 159295 trillion yuan. Expenditure in Quarter 1 was relatively lower, caused by the system of the budget approved by the people's congress; government expenditure increased gradually in Quarter 2 and 3, and sharply in Quarter 4, almost two times of that in Quarter 1. In addition, on a monthly basis, government expenditure in the last month of each quarter was greater than that in the first two months, that is, expenditure in March, June, September and December was high, respectively accounting for the highest ratio in the current quarter. Particularly, government expenditure in December was 2. 081595 trillion, up to 16.6% [1] in total expenditure throughout the year. This reflects that the phenomenon of quarters-end or year-end "crash expenditure" was popular with all departments and units under the budget management. Additionally, the table also lists monthly growths of government expenditure. Compared with that in 2011, monthly growths and growth rates of government expenditure were largely increased mainly caused by huge pressures of expenditure in key areas, such as education, medical and health care, social security and government-subsidized housing.

Table 3.13 Monthly National Government Expenditure and Its Growth in 2012

(Unit: 100 million yuan, %)

Month	Government expenditure completed	Growth over last year	Year-on-year growth rate	Percentage
1-2	13924.14	3440.57	32.8	11.1
3	10193.91	2623.91	34.7	8.1
4	7885	581	8	6.3
5	9165	897	10.8	7.3
6	12724	1915	17.7	10.1
7	9528	2578	37.1	7.6
8	9020	943	11.7	7.2
9	11679	1660	16.6	9.3
10	8617	538	6.7	6.9
11	12160	764	6.7	9.7
12	20815.95	546	2.7	16.6
Total	125712	16464	15.1	–

Source: the website of the Ministry of Finance.

[1] Despite of this, the percentage was reduced by 3.7 percentage points in 2010 and 2 in 2011 respectively. As time passes on, China's fiscal expenditure is becoming more balanced.

3.4.2 Structure of government expenditure by items

The 12th Five-year Plan period is significant for China to boost optimization and upgrading of its industrial structure and transformation of its economic growth pattern. In 2012, the second year to implement the 12th Five-year Plan, the financial department continued to implement a proactive fiscal policy tightly around the theme of scientific development and accelerating transformation of the economic growth mode, with priorities on adjusting the distribution pattern of national income, promoting the reform of fiscal and taxation system and optimizing the structure of fiscal expenditure. Items of China's government expenditure in 2012 are shown in Table 3.14.

Table 3.14 Items of Public Finance Expenditure in 2012①

(Unit: 100 million yuan, %)

Item	Figure implemented	Growth rate	Ranking by growth rate	Percentage	Ranking by percentage
Total national fiscal expenditures	125712	15.1	–	–	–
General public services	–	–	–	–	–
diplomacy	–	–	–	–	–
national defense	–	–	–	–	–
public security	–	–	–	–	–
education	21165	28.3	1	16.8	1
science and technology	4429	15.7	6	3.5	7
culture, sports and media	2251	18.9	3	1.8	10
social security and employment	12542	12.9	7	10	2
medical and health care	7199	12	8	5.7	6
energy conservation and environmental protection	2932	11	9	2.3	9
urban and rural community affairs	9020	18.4	4	7.2	4

① Rankings by the growth rate and percentage are only based on data available.

Item	Figure implemented	Growth rate	Ranking by growth rate	Percentage	Ranking by percentage
agriculture, forestry and water conservancy affairs	11903	19.8	2	9.5	3
transportation	8713	9	10	6.9	5
resource exploration, electricity and information affairs	–	–	–	–	–
commercial and service industry affairs	–	–	–	–	–
financial regulation affairs	–	–	–	–	–
post-earthquake restoration and reconstruction	–	–	–	–	–
Land and meteorological affairs	–	–	–	–	–
guaranteeing adequate housing	4446	16.4	5	3.5	7
grain, edible oils, and other materials reserve affairs	–	–	–	–	–
interest payment for national debts	–	–	–	–	–
other expenditure	–	–	–	–	–

Source: the website of the Ministry of Finance. " – " indicates that data of the corresponding item are not obtained.

It can be known from the table that: First, the financial department increased supports for expenditure on people's livelihood, including education, science and technology, culture, sports and media, medical and health care, social security and government-subsidized housing. In 2012, national fiscal spending on education stood at 2.1165 trillion yuan, up 28.3%, ranking No. 1 and accounting for up to 16.4% in national fiscal expenditure, also ranking No.1. Spending on social security and employment reached 1.2542 trillion yuan, accounting for up to 10% in national fiscal expenditure, the second largest spending on people's livelihood only second to education. In addition, growths of spending on science and technology, culture, sports and media, medical and health care and government-subsidized housing were above 10% respectively. Increased expenditure on people's livelihood, especially that provide more benefits for small and medium wages earners, helped adjust the distribution pattern of national income and narrow the gap of income distribution. Second, increased expenditure on science and technology, energy conservation and environmental protection that help realize the adjustment of industrial structure and transform the economic growth pattern. In 2012, spending on energy conservation and environmental protection stood at 293. 2 billion yuan, up 11%. In addition, increased investment on medical care, pension insurance and public services helped accelerate upgrading of the industrial structure. Third, increased spending on agriculture, forestry and water conservancy, and spending on urban and rural community affairs that aimed to balance urban and rural development. In 2012, spending on agriculture, forestry and water conservancy reached 1. 1903 trillion yuan, up 19. 8%, which was only second to education, and accounted for a high proportion of 9. 5%; spending on urban and rural community affairs increased sharply to 18. 4%, with a proportion of 7. 2%. As both spending on agriculture, forestry and water conservancy and spending on urban and rural community affairs are closely related to the issue of agriculture, farmers and rural areas, their rapid growths and high proportions indicates that the Chinese government attaches great importance to solving the issue of agriculture, farmers and rural areas.

To sum up, we can see that in 2012, China's fiscal expenditure has provided a positive guide for advancing adjustment of the industrial structure, realizing transformation of the economic growth pattern, regulating distribution of national income and achieving sustainable social and economic development.

3. 4. 3 Structure of government expenditure by governments at different levels

Table 3. 15 shows the amounts and proportions of expenditure by central government and local governments in 2001 to 2012. It can be known from the table that: the amount of expenditure by both central and local governments has been on the rise year after year. Central government expenditure rose up from 576. 802 billion yuan in 2001 to 1. 9765 trillion yuan in 2012, while local governments expenditure in the same period climbed up from 1. 313456 trillion yuan to 10. 6947 trillion yuan. In terms of the proportion in total expenditure, from 2001 to 2012, the proportion of central government expenditure continued to decline from 30.5% in 2001 to 14.9% in 2012, while that of local governments expenditure in the same period grew up year by year from 69.5% to 85.1%. Such an expenditure structure combined with the huge proportion of central government revenue in total national fiscal revenue explains that: transfer payments from central government to local governments have been substantial and tends to increase constantly. Increased transfer payments from the central government shall, on one hand, be good to promote balance between regions, and on the other, indicate that control of the central government has been intensified. That is, "centralization" of fiscal powers has been increasingly enhanced since establishment of the tax-sharing system, which is potentially ill to improving initiatives of local governments.

Table 3. 15 Amounts and Proportions of Central and Local Governments expenditure

Year	Absolute figure (100 million yuan)			Percentage (%)	
	National	Central government	Local governments	Central government	Local governments
2001	18902.58	5768.02	13134.56	30.5	69.5
2002	22053.15	6771.7	15281.45	30.7	69.3
2003	24649.95	7420.1	17229.85	30.1	69.9
2004	28486.89	7894.08	20592.81	27.7	72.3
2005	33930.28	8775.97	25154.31	25.9	74.1
2006	40422.73	9991.4	30431.33	24.7	75.3
2007	49781.35	11442.06	38339.29	23	77
2008	62592.66	13344.17	49248.49	21.3	78.7
2009	76299.93	15255.79	61044.14	20	80
2010	89874.16	15989.73	73884.43	17.8	82.2
2011	108930	16514	92416	15.2	84.8
2012	125712	18765	106947	14.93	85.1

Notes: Data obtained through calculation after taken from the website of the Ministry of Finance and Finance Yearbook of China.

3.5 Analysis on Major Fiscal Expenditure Items in 2012

In 2012, China's government continued to make significant appropriations for improving people's livelihood. Based on central fiscal budgets, governments at all levels were to concentrate financial resources to accomplish 6 major tasks aimed at maintaining and improving living standards in 2012. First, further increase education spending to ensure budgetary expenditure on education nationwide accounts for 4% of GDP. Second, accelerate the development of the social security system, and make the new old-age insurance system available to all eligible rural and urban residents. Third, deepen reform of the pharmaceutical and healthcare systems, increase government subsidies to the new rural cooperative medical care system and basic medical insurance for urban residents, speed up trial reforms in public hospitals, and make medical services more affordable and accessible. Fourth, make steady progress in building low-income housing, begin construction on more than seven million units of housing while completing ongoing projects, and help ease housing difficulties of low-income urban residents, first-time workers, and rural migrant workers. Fifth, vigorously promote cultural development and prosperity, and ensure that growth in government spending on cultural development exceeds the regular revenue increase, in order to better satisfy people's cultural needs. Sixth, increase policy support to strengthen agriculture, benefit farmers, and make the countryside prosperous; support construction of irrigation and water conservancy facilities and other working and living infrastructure in rural areas; and stimulate innovation in agricultural science and technology. Therefore, spending on education, spending on social security and employment, spending on medical and health care, spending on guaranteeing adequate housing, spending on culture, sports and media, and spending for supporting agriculture were major expenditure items in 2012.

3.5.1 Spending on education

Spending on education is a fundamental and strategic investment to support long-term development of the country, and constitutes material foundations of education. Giving top priority to education is an important function of public finance. Over years, financial departments at various levels have taken positive measures to further increase inputs on education, strive to widen sources of government spending on education, and boost educational reform and development. The ratio of national spending on education to GDP has been raised year by year, and spending on education has become the largest expenditure of public finance.

In 2012, financial departments at various levels fulfilled legal requirements for growth of government spending on education, and further increased financial inputs in education. To sum up fiscal budgets, expenditure from government-managed funds on education and other government spending on education, national spending on education in 2012 reached 2.198463 trillion yuan, accounting for above 4% of GDP. This is the first time for China to achieve the strategic objective put forward in 1993 that national spending on education shall be raided to account for 4% of GDP.

First of all, the central government continued to expand inputs in education. In 2012, the appropriation for education was 378.132 billion yuan, an increase of 16.4%. This consisted of 102.887 billion yuan of spending at the central level and 275.245 billion yuan in transfer payments to local governments. Firstly, the central government planned to allocate 15 billion yuan, up 48.1%, in subsidies to implement a host of policies and measures for promoting the development of preschool education, with the focus on the central and western regions and poor areas of the eastern region. Secondly, 105.754 billion yuan was planned to be allocated to improve the mechanism for guaranteeing funding for rural compulsory education, push forward upgrading of weak rural compulsory education schools, implement the plan to attract exemplary teachers to work in rural compulsory education schools and the state programs to train primary and secondary school teachers, and promote balanced development of compulsory education. 16 billion yuan was to be disbursed in rewards and subsidies to carry out an initiative designed to improve the nutrition of rural students attending compulsory education schools in contiguous areas with particular difficulties. Thirdly, 8.2 billion yuan was to be earmarked to exempt urban compulsory education students from tuition and miscellaneous fees, and make compulsory education equally available to children of rural migrant workers in cities. Fourthly, China planned to allocate 25.68 billion yuan, up 91.7%, to further strengthen vocational education infrastructure and phase in a system to make secondary vocational education free of charge; 20.697 billion yuan in subsidies to improve the policy system for providing government financial aid to students from poor families. Fifthly, the central government planned to allocate 135.25 billion yuan, up 24%, to advance Project 985 and Project 211 and support the development of local colleges and universities. In addition, local governments allocated 1.790024 trillion yuan, up 18.4%, to spend on education.

3.5.2 Spending on social security and employment

A perfect social security system provides significant guarantees for maintaining social stability and long-term national stability. In recent years, financial departments have strengthened supports for social security and employment and achieved good results. For example, coverage of the new type of endowment insurance for rural residents was extended to more than 60% of China's counties, basic pensions for enterprise retirees were increased for the seventh consecutive year, and the system of putting basic pension insurance for enterprise employees under unified planning at the provincial level was further improved. Additionally, the mechanism to link the standard for social rescue and guarantee with price increases was established throughout China, and the policy to provide subsidies and living allowances for some entitled groups was implemented.

In 2012, the appropriation for social security and employment was 575.073 billion yuan, an increase of 21.9%. This figure consisted of 57.063 billion yuan of spending at the central level and 518.01 billion yuan in transfer payments to local governments. China planned to allocate 77.1 billion yuan in subsidies to ensure all eligible rural and urban residents are covered by the new endowment insurance system by July 1, 2012. 217.373 billion yuan was to be appropriated in subsidies to continue to increase basic pension benefits of enterprise retirees and improve the overall planning system for basic retirement pension funds for enterprise employees at the provincial level. 92.888 billion yuan was to be appropriated to raise subsistence allowances to a suitable level, with per capita monthly benefits to be increased by 15 and 12 yuan for urban and rural recipients respectively, and to further improve social assistance systems targeted at orphans, people with disabilities, vagrants, and beggars. 28.837 billion yuan was to be disbursed to raise subsidies and living allowances for entitled groups as needed, 13 billion yuan to guarantee basic living conditions of disaster victims, and 43. 917 billion yuan to increase policy support for employment. The same year, spending by local governments on social security and employment amounted to 1. 236729 trillion yuan, up 16. 2%.

3. 5. 3 Spending on medical and health care

As one of major issues related to people's livelihood, the cause of medical and health care concerns the health of billions of people and happiness of thousands of households. Since the launch of the medical reform in April 2009, financial departments at various government levels have optimized their structures of fiscal expenditures and constantly increased inputs in medical and health care, which provided strong capital guarantees to successfully push forward the medical reform. From 2009 to 2011, national fiscal spending on medical and health care totaled 1. 5166 trillion yuan, including 450. 6 billion yuan contributed by the central government. Compared by the same standard, during the three years, national spending increased by 1. 2409 trillion yuan, a growth of 390. 9 billion yuan over the target of 850 billion yuan, while central government spending grew up by 368 billion yuan, 36. 2 billion yuan higher than the target of 331. 8 billion yuan. Over the three years, key medical reform tasks were smoothly accomplished. Almost all urban and rural residents have been covered by the basic medical insurance system, and the government subsidies for basic medical insurance for urban residents and the new type of rural cooperative medical care system were raised to no less than 200 yuan per capita per year, and about 70% of hospital fees covered by the policy can be reimbursed.

In 2012, financial departments at various levels increased inputs on medical and health care, improved methods for evaluation of fund performances and strengthened supervision of financial funds and medical insurance funds, and vigorously advanced key medical reform tasks. The appropriation arranged by the central finance for medical and health care was 203. 505 billion yuan, an increase of 16. 4%. This figure consisted of 8. 331 billion yuan of spending at the central level and 195. 174 billion yuan in transfer payments to local governments, a gain of 16. 8% from the figure completed in 2011. Central government spending om community-level medical and health care institutions had the largest growth, up by 33.9% over that in 2011, mainly caused by increased spending on infrastructure construction. The budget planned to allocate 105 billion yuan in subsidies, up 37%, to raise government subsidies for the new rural cooperative medical care system and basic medical insurance for urban residents to 240 yuan per person per year, and appropriately increase the proportion of costs that are reimbursable. Efforts were to be made to improve the national system of basic drugs, and deepen the comprehensive reform of community-level medical and health care institutions. 35.8 billion yuan was to be allocated to improve the mechanism for ensuring funding for delivering basic public health services to rural and urban residents, and continue to implement basic public health programs and prevent and control major communicable diseases such as AIDS and tuberculosis. Trial reforms were to be accelerated in public hospitals, with particular focus on county-level hospitals. Supports were planned for the work of providing medical assistance to rural and urban residents with an appropriation of 11.483 billion yuan. In the same year, spending on medical and health care arranged by local finances totaled 726.46 billion yuan, up 15.4%.

3.5.4 Spending on guaranteeing adequate housing

The Chinese government and the Communist Party of China insisted on the housing policy that struggles to make more people, especially those with low incomes, "own a house". Since 2008, the Chinese government has accelerated the construction of government-subsidized housing, and put it at the top of ten measures to expand domestic demands. In particular, the budgeted figure for central government spending on guaranteeing adequate housing saw substantial growth since 2010. The Chinese government started to build 5.8 million units of government-subsidized housing in 2010, 10 million units in 2011 and 7 million in 2012. Though the total number of units of government-subsidized housing started to build in 2012 were reduced slightly from the 10 million units in last year, , the actual construction work in progress was enormous and the construction funds actually invested shall be more than that in the past 5 years. In 2012, the appropriation arranged by the central government for guaranteeing adequate housing was 211.755 billion yuan, an increase of 23.1%. This figure consisted of 37.44 billion yuan of spending at the central level and 174.315 billion yuan in transfer payments to local governments. 178. 746 billion yuan, an increase of 24. 8% , was appropriated to build low-income housing projects, appropriately expand the scope of dilapidated rural houses eligible for policy-backed renovation and raise the standard of subsidies from the central government, and steadily push forward the construction of permanent housing for nomads. Of the same year, spending on guaranteeing adequate housing arranged by local finances amounted to 402. 4 billion yuan, a growth of 15. 2%.

3.5.5 Spending on culture, sports and media

As the blood vessel of a nation, culture functions as the spiritual garden for its people. The Sixth Plenary Session of the Seventeenth Central Committee of the Communist Party of China made significant arrangements to deepen reform of the cultural system, promoting the great development and flourishing of socialist culture. In order to support construction of an institutional mechanism for cultural development and flourishing to promote the great development and flourishing of socialist culture, financial departments increased government spending on culture and gave priorities to fulfill the following 4 tasks:

First, establish a mechanism for stable growth of government spending on culture. Efforts were made to ensure that the growth of public finance investment in cultural construction is higher than the growth of regular national revenue and raise the proportion of spending on culture in national expenditure. Sources of government spending on culture were further expanded to encourage and guide various organizations and individuals to participate in cultural construction, and increase government inputs in culture from non-tax revenue.

Second, intensify guarantees for spending on key cultural areas. A long-term mechanism for guaranteeing the supply of public cultural services was established and improved to incorporate major public cultural products, services, and activities into the budget for regular government expenditure. Supports were provided to protect and inherit excellent traditional culture, the guide for creation and production of cultural products shall be enhanced, and supports for the Chinese culture to " go abroad" shall be provided to improve communication and influence of the Chinese culture.

Third, offer supports to deepen reform of the cultural system. More efforts were made to guarantee funds for nonprofit cultural organizations, study and formulate management regulations for institutional organizations, including ordinary magazines and newspapers focusing on politics and key cultural institutions and groups, to run like enterprises. Special funds for development of the cultural industry were largely increased to boost transformation of newspapers and magazines not focusing on politics and ordinary cultural institutions and groups into enterprises. Supports were provided to implement the strategy of developing major cultural industrial projects, and efforts shall be made to develop new media and new forms of cultural operations, accelerate cultivation of key enterprises and support exports of cultural products and services.

Fourth, enhance management of state-owned cultural assets. Efforts were made to explore and improve the management system of state-owned cultural assets, establish and perfect the institutions and working mechanism for supervision and management of state-owned cultural assets. Management methods were developed to supervise state-owned assets of central cultural enterprises, enhance management of state-owned assets during transformation of cultural units into enterprises and promote optimization and restructuring of state-owned cultural assets.

To this end, the central finance appropriated 49.384 billion yuan, up 18.7%, for culture, sports and media in 2012. This figure consisted of 20.733 billion yuan of spending at the central level and 28.651 billion yuan in transfer payments to local governments. According to the budget plan, 14.546 billion yuan was to be allocated to develop the system of public cultural services, support free admission to public cultural facilities such as museums and public libraries, and continue to implement key cultural projects that benefit the people. 6.124 billion yuan, up 40%, was appropriated to strengthen protection of key national cultural artifacts, major cultural and historical sites, cultural resources related to the early history of the CPC, and intangible cultural heritage; 2.75 billion yuan, up 37.5%, to strengthen the international broadcasting capability of key media and support efforts to take Chinese culture to a global audience; and 3.4 billion yuan, up 70%, to support the development of the culture industry. Simultaneously, spending on culture, sports and media arranged by local finances reached 197.151 billion yuan, a gain of 15.9%.

3.5.6 Fiscal expenditure to support agriculture

The issue of agriculture, farmers and rural areas is fundamental to China's overall economic and social development. Financial departments have insisted on giving top priority to solving the issue of agriculture, farmers and rural areas. As pointed out by the No. 1 central document of 2012, the basic way to realize sustainable and steady growth of agriculture to ensure effective supply of agricultural products over a long period lies in science and technology. To accelerate innovations of agricultural science and technology and advance construction of modern agriculture, financial departments at various levels focused on "building the mechanism, increasing investment, strengthening science and technology and promoting agricultural production" to further support establishment and improvement of the service system for promoting agricultural technology and boost the steady development of agricultural production in line with requirements by the central government and on the basis of integrating existing sources of government funds. In 2012, expenditure on agriculture, farmers and rural areas by the central government totaled 1. 22866 trillion yuan, up 17.9%; local governments also increased inputs in agriculture, farmers and rural areas, mainly focusing on the following aspects:

First, provide supports for research and development of agricultural science and technology. More supports were provided for fundamental, nonprofit and leading scientific research of agriculture. Supports were continued for implementing major projects to cultivate new varieties of genetically modified organisms, national science and technology plans for agriculture, and special projects of natural science fund, key national laboratories, and nonprofit research institutions, special action plan to enrich people and strengthen counties, and the plan to benefit farmers and flourish villages with scientific knowledge.

Second, provide supports for promotion and services of agricultural science and technology. Efforts were made to improve construction of the system of agricultural production technology and services, advance reform of the grassroots system to promote agricultural technology and construction of model counties, enhance promotion of agricultural technology and raise contributions of agricultural science and technology to agricultural production, promote and adopt the technology to breed superior crop varieties, prevent and reduce disasters in the agricultural field, and increased training of grassroots workers promoting agricultural technology and farmers.

Third, improve the mechanical equipments of agriculture. The central government continued to increase subsidies for purchase of agricultural machinery, and further optimize the structure of subsidies for purchase of agricultural machinery by incorporating mechanical machineries for animal husbandry, forestry, drought-resisting and water-saving into subsidies. More supports were provided for solving the bottleneck of agricultural mechanization in rice planting and harvest of corn, sugarcane and rapeseed to promote the level of agricultural machinery and productivity.

Expenditures closely related to expenditures on "Agriculture, farmers and rural areas" include spending on agriculture, forestry and water conservancy and expenditure on grain, edible oils and other materials reserve affairs. In 2012, the central finance appropriated 549. 145 billion yuan, up 14. 8% , for agriculture, forestry and water conservancy. This figure consisted of 42. 744 billion yuan of spending at the central level and 506. 401 billion yuan in transfer payments to local governments. Efforts were made to advance the construction of small irrigation and water conservancy facilities in key counties, appropriately raise construction and subsidy standards, and intensify efforts to harness small and medium-sized rivers, reinforce dangerously defective small reservoirs, and prevent and control geological disasters due to mountain torrents. Altogether, allocations for agricultural and rural infrastructure development stood at 165. 446 billion yuan. 169. 338 billion yuan was appropriated to improve the policy on subsidies for superior crop varieties, scale up general subsidies for agricultural supplies and subsidies for the purchase of agricultural machinery, increase the areas and crop varieties eligible for subsidies on agricultural insurance premiums, and further increase subsidies for afforestation. 10. 1 billion yuan, up 53% , was earmarked to increase funding for agricultural science and technology, improve the environment for fostering innovations in this area, develop a modern seed industry and a system for spreading agricultural technologies in villages, translate advances in agricultural science and technology into practical productive forces, and promote wider application of agricultural technology. 29. 012 billion yuan was allocated to strengthen comprehensive agricultural development, with the focus on main grain-growing areas and major grain-producing counties. The subsidy and award policy for grassland ecological conservation was fully implemented with an allocation of 15.058 billion yuan. Investment in comprehensive poverty relief efforts was significantly increased to enhance self-development capabilities of rural poverty-stricken areas and the poor population, and 37.286 billion yuan of special government funds will be used to support these efforts, up 18.7%. 24.8 billion yuan was appropriated in subsidies to continue to implement the government award and subsidy system for village-level public works projects, the launching of which is determined by villagers themselves, and to improve the mechanism of village-level public service projects being run by villagers and subsidized by the government. Spending on agriculture, forestry and water conservancy by local governments amounted to 1.081678 trillion yuan, up 14.2%.

Moreover, the central finance appropriated 97.419 billion yuan, up 9.4%, for grain, edible oils and other materials reserve affairs. This figure consisted of 60.957 billion yuan of spending at the central level and 36.462 billion yuan in transfer payments to local governments. China continued to implement the policy of direct grain subsidies, and earmarked 32.03 billion yuan for grain risk funds. Efforts were also made to improve systems for purchasing and grain, cotton, and other main agricultural products reserve, steadily raise the minimum purchase prices of wheat and rice with 51.876 billion yuan allocated for reserves of grain, edible oils and other important materials.

3.6 Conclusions and Outlooks

3.6.1 Conclusions

The year of 2012 was gone. To look back, under the keynote of "continuing implementing a proactive fiscal policy, improving the policy of structural tax reduction increasing inputs on people's livelihood, promoting economic restructuring, tightening revenue and expenditure management, and enhancing management of local governments debts", government expenditure in 2012 had the following characteristics:

First, the growth rate of government expenditure dropped sharply, but its percentage in GDP continued to increase. In 2012, national fiscal expenditure totaled 12.5712 trillion yuan, up 1.6464 trillion yuan or 15.1%, or 6.5 percentage points lower than that of 2011, only higher than that in 2003 since 2002, a sharp decline in the growth rate of government expenditure. In addition, national fiscal expenditure exceeded national fiscal revenue, resulting in a budget deficit of 850. 2 billion yuan, a growth of 312. 86 billion yuan over the previous year. Besides, the growth of national expenditure was higher than of revenue. Since 2002, fiscal expenditure only grew up faster than fiscal revenue in 3 years, namely, 2008, 2009 and 2012, reflecting the efforts the government has made to use the proactive fiscal policy to stimulate the economy in recent years. Though the growth of government expenditure reduced sharply, the ratio of government expenditure to GDP has been increased constantly and hit the historic high of 24. 2% since 2000, indicating that the government continuously deepened participation in the economic life. It should be pointed out that though government stimulus to the economy can boost economic growth within a certain period, this kind of growth shall not be sustainable if participation of private capitals is not expanded.

Second, the strength of government expenditure climbed up and the proportion of expenditure on people's livelihood continued to increase. We use government expenditure/government revenue ratio to measure the strength of fiscal expenditure. Data reveal that though growth rates of government expenditure and revenue declined sharply in 2012, the strength of fiscal expenditure turned to increase slightly. In 2012, the strength of government expenditure was 1. 07, exceeding 1. 05 of 2011. Based on specific expenditure items, government expenditure in 2012 focused more on people's livelihood. Throughout the year, expenditure on people's livelihood accounted for 63. 34% of government expenditure, 1. 4 percentage points higher than the previous year[1]. Of all expenditure items, spending on education, spending on social security and employment, spending on medical and health care, spending on guaranteeing adequate housing, spending on culture, sports and media, and expenditure to support agriculture, farmers and rural areas were priorities of expenditure on people's livelihood in 2012. This is mainly because the central economic work conference held at the beginning of 2012 re-

---

[1] Data are obtained through calculation after taken from the website of the Ministry of Finance.

strengthened the importance of a proactive fiscal policy and expenditure on people's livelihood.

Third, transparency of government expenditure waits to be improved and budget management needs to be enhanced. Based on the government expenditure report system, China has formed a preliminary budget system for the budgets of public finance, government-managed funds and state capital operations. However, as of 2012, the budget of national social insurance funds has not been officially developed and the budget of state capital operations only includes financial information of less than 10% of funds owned by state-owned enterprises. As for the budgets of public finance and government-managed funds, expenditure information revealed are more of categories classified by functions than details, and almost no information can be found to be classified by economic natures. Limited fiscal transparency to a great degree affects supervision of the National People's Congress and the public over the government's fiscal activities, leading to ineffective use of a great part of financial capitals. Therefore, it is necessary to further increase fiscal transparency and tighten budget management to create conditions for the people's congress and the public to oversee the use of financial capitals.

3.6.2 Outlooks for 2013

The central economic work conference held at the beginning of 2013 re-strengthened the importance of a proactive fiscal policy and expenditure on people's livelihood. To better make use of the proactive fiscal policy in maintaining growth, adjusting the structure, promoting reform and benefiting people's life, we predict government expenditure arranged in 2013 shall have the following characteristics:

First, the growth of government expenditure shall continue to reduce and the budget deficit will be further increased. Affected by uncertainties and instabilities in international trade, slowdown of growth potentials faced by domestic demands to realize rapid growth and decline in revenue growth, the growth of China's government expenditure in 2013 shall further drop. In terms of the total amount, government expenditure in 2013 shall exceed government revenue, causing the budget deficit to increase compared with 2012, mainly because: Structural tax reduction shall produce a lag effect, so that the growth of government revenue in 2013 shall not be too fast. But rigid government expenditure continues to increase, particularly expenditure on protecting and improving people's livelihood, solidifying the fundamental position of agriculture, and maintaining supports for economic growth and restructuring, so it is required to increase the budget deficit and the size of government bonds.

Second, the structure of government expenditure shall be further optimized with the proportion of expenditures on people's livelihood further increased, mainly because: on one side, government expenditure shall continue to increase in areas related to people's livelihood and weak links, including education, medical and health care, and social security. In 2012, government spending on education increased to 4% of GDP for the first time in China. Therefore, we can predict that it should not be less than 4% and may be even greater in 2013, that is, total spending on education shall be greater. In addition to spending on education, growths of expenditures on other items directly related to people's life, including medical and health care, social security and employment, government-subsidized housing, and culture, shall be great. Investment in the central government budget shall be made mainly in government-subsidized housing, infrastructure of agriculture, water conservancy and urban pipeline network, social programs and other projects for people's livelihood, energy saving and emission reduction, and protection of the ecological environment, therefore, expenditure on people's livelihood shall continue to increase in proportion. On the other, administrative overheads including spending on administrative management shall be reduced. In 2012, the General Office of the State Council released Regulations on Administration of Government Offices, making restrictions to expenditure on administration of government offices, such as vehicle purchases and maintenance, overseas trips and official receptions, government procurement management and conference management. Therefore, it can be predicted that the proportion of administrative overheads shall be reduced. It can be seen that the structure of China's government expenditure in 2013 will be further enhanced. In addition, expenditures on "agriculture, farmer and rural areas" shall remain a priority of government expenditure in 2013, mainly because: In recent years, the Central Committee of the Communist Party of China and the State Council have developed a series of policies to boost agriculture, benefit farmers and increase rural prosperity, giving top priority to solving issues related to "agriculture, farmers and rural areas". In the past 5 years, central government expenditure on "agriculture, farmers and rural areas" totaled 4. 47 trillion yuan, an average annual growth of 23. 5% , up by 2. 92 trillion yuan from the previous five years. Therefore, China shall further increase inputs on "agriculture, farmers and rural areas" in 2013, to gradually establish a new type of system for intensive agricultural operations that are specialized, well organized and commercialized by establishing a sound system for subsidizing grain farmers and a sound mechanism for subsidizing major grain-producing areas, carrying out the policy of minimum grain purchase prices, making greater progress in agricultural science and technology and the development of modern agriculture, and to achieve a new type of relations between industry and agriculture and between urban and rural areas in which industry promotes agriculture, urban areas support rural development, agriculture and industry benefit each other and urban areas are integrated with rural areas by promoting integrated urban and rural development.

Third, the structure of transfer payments shall be further optimized and the government budget system shall be more improved. Based on the experience of increasing the size of general transfer payments and raising its proportion in the past 5 years[1], the proportion of general transfer payments in China's transfer payments shall be further raised in 2013. At the same time, more efforts shall be made to group and sort out special transfer payments so that the structure of transfer payments can be optimized. Correspondingly, central government's transfer payments to local governments shall become local governments revenue to be allocated by local governments for expenditures on protecting and improving people's livelihood, thus effectively promote equalization of fundamental public services and balanced development between regions. Moreover, in terms of the government budget system, China shall formally establish a budget for national social security funds for the first time in 2013, and the Report issued at the 18th National Congress of the Communist Party of China clearly points out that China will "refine the government budget system and bring all government receipts and expenditures under budg-

---

[1] From 2007 to 2012, the proportion of general transfer payments in total transfer payments climbed up from 50. 8% in 2007 to 53. 3% in 2012.

etary management···". Thus, we can predict that in 2013, the Chinese government shall take actions to improve the budget system for government-managed funds and state-owned capital operations, and establish an institutional framework and a set of standards for the budget management of social insurance funds.

References:

1. Report on the Implementation of Central and Local Budgets for 2011 and on Draft Central and Local Budgets for 2012, http://www. gov. cn/2012lh/content_2093446. htm

2. Final Accounts of National Revenue and Expenditures in 2011, http://yss. mof. gov. cn/2011qgczjs/index. html.

3. National Fiscal Revenue and Expenditure in 2012, http://www. mof. gov. cn/zhengwuxinxi/redianzhuanti/quanguocaizhengshouzhiqingkuang/

4. The Ministry of Finance of the People's Republic of China: http://www. mof. gov. cn/

5. National Bureau of Statistics of China: http://www. stats. gov. cn/

6. Zeng Junping, Liu Xiaobing, Report on China's Public Finance 2012, Peking University Press, 2012.

7. Center for Public Policy Studies of Shanghai University of Finance and Economics, Report on China's Fiscal Transparency 2012, Shanghai University of Finance and Economics Press, 2012.

4 Econometric Analysis of China's Public Finance

4.1 Overview

In this chapter, we shall adopt econometric models to analyze and evaluate China's fiscal regime. Despite of a list of problems in modeling, such as non-sequence of time series data, inconsistence of statistic scope, time delay and erogeneity of macroeconomic variables, which cause it much difficult to establish a complete system of econometric models for fiscal and economic calculations. Such attempt, however, can depict the motion path, change patterns and mutual impacts of major variables in China's fiscal and economic system.

Strong operation of the public finance plays a significant role in economic and social development. As one of major ways to realize macroeconomic control, the public finance is very important in optimizing resource allocation. By controlling total amount and directions of fiscal revenue and expenditures, it is good to optimize balance and structure of aggregate social demands and supplies, ensure the sustainable, rapid and healthy development of the national economy. Public finance can energetically promote the development of science, education, culture and health. Meantime, it makes a broad adjustment of social allocation by taxation and spending on social security to play a positive role in promoting economic growth and elevating people's living standard. So it is safe to say that public finances involve all aspects of a country's economic and social development. Handling and analysis of fiscal issues often require substantial combination with practical data. So it is far from enough to analyze fiscal problems only from a qualitative perspective. Quantitative analysis remains a must to comprehensively understand fiscal problems. A continu-

ous econometric analysis of the fiscal regime through models can present an o-
verall description and forecast of future values, scope and tendencies of key
variables of the fiscal and economic system, so as to command the general operation laws of China's fiscal and economic system to provide a theoretic basis
for formulating relative fiscal and taxation policies.

During the model design, in order to analyze accuracy of the forecasts after the design, we have basically ensured that indicators selected for the forecasts have the same statistical coverage with those of official statistics and done
our best to clarify variables for China's fiscal econometric models. In setting
model structures and behavioral equations, we have tried our best to keep in
line with the practical operation process and structure of China's fiscal and e-
conomic system. As for the modeling method, we have adopted the co-integration theory under time series and co-integration analysis of panel data in addition to traditional least squares. If the data remain stable, least squares shall
be used. If the data turn to be a unit root process, co-integration shall be
used to estimate and equivalent error to correct the estimate.

Part Two of this chapter makes a brief introduction to basic modeling
principles, methods and data. Part Three briefly explains settings of econometric models and Part Four is assigned to exhibit results of fiscal and taxation
econometric analyses.

4.2 Basic ideas, methods and data for building economic models

Generally speaking, there are two ideas about building economic models:
one is to adopt the method of mathematical analysis based on mechanism (or
theoretical) analysis and guided by economic theories to describe conservation
law or causal relationship between key factors of the economic system and in-
tentionally depict the correlation between these factors and mechanism for their
mutual influence so as to reflect operations of the economic system; the other
is to mainly use time data or spatial data of key factors of the economic system
to describe relevance and causal relationship between all factors through econometric tools such as time series or panel data analysis so as to reflect change
patterns and mutual influence between key indicators or variables of the eco-

nomic system in time and space. Presently, both modeling ideas tend to integrate each other. In other words, it is not comprehensive and objective to reveal the complicated operating mechanism of the economic system only by mechanism or data analysis.

As to the economitric method, in consideration of spurious regression and economic inertia of time series, we adopt the following method: to reduce data fluctuations, logarithm of level values of the variables is taken and differentiated. The ADF testing method is utilized to test variable stationarity of time series. Unstable series are assessed through linear co-integration, given correction for its error.

It should be pointed out that due to fiscal expenditures substantially reclassified in 2007, we adopt monthly data after 2007 for analysis in econometric analysis models of fiscal expenditures. In addition, the fiscal econometric analysis models do not include equations for extra-budgetary revenue and expenditures. And STATA 11.2 and RATS 8.0 are used for econometric modeling and data analysis while data are taken from the database of CEI Statistics Database and DRCnet database of the State Council. (See details in Table 4.1)

Table 4.1 Data Sources

Data	Source
Annual total fiscal revenue (1979 ~ 2011)	DRCnet Database of the State Council
Annual total tax revenue (1979 ~ 2011)	DRCnet Database of the State Council
Annual central government revenue (1980 ~ 2011)	DRCnet Database of the State Council
Annual local governments revenue (1980 ~ 2011)	DRCnet Database of the State Council
Annual GDP (1978 ~ 2011)	DRCnet Database of the State Council
Annual added values of the secondary industry (1980 ~ 2011)	DRCnet Database of the State Council
Annual added values of the tertiary industry (1980 ~ 2011)	DRCnet Database of the State Council
Annul industrial added values (1985 ~ 2011)	DRCnet Database of the State Council
Annual revenue from value-added tax (1985 ~ 2011)	DRCnet Database of the State Council

Data	Source
Annual revenue from business tax (1985 ~ 2011)	DRCnet Database of the State Council
Annual revenue from customs duties (1985 ~ 2011)	DRCnet Database of the State Council
Annual retail sales of consumer goods (1985 ~ 2011)	DRCnet Database of the State Council
Annual total fiscal expenditures (1978 ~ 2011)	DRCnet Database of the State Council
Annual central government expenditures (1978 ~ 2011)	DRCnet Database of the State Council
Annual local governments expenditures (1978 ~ 2011)	DRCnet Database of the State Council
Monthly spending on general public services (2007. 1 ~ 2012. 12)	CEI Statistics Database
Monthly spending on education (2007. 1 ~ 2012. 12)	CEI Statistics Database
Monthly spending on science and technology (2007. 1 ~ 2012. 12)	CEI Statistics Database
Monthly spending on social security (2007. 1 ~ 2012. 12)	CEI Statistics Database
Monthly spending on environment protection (2007. 1 ~ 2012. 12)	CEI Statistics Database

4.3 Settings of Econometric Models for China's Public Finance

4.3.1 Econometric models for fiscal revenue

Econometric models of fiscal revenue include aggregate model and revenue growth model.

4.3.1.1 Total revenue model is designed with 8 equations

(1) − 1 Equation about relationship between total fiscal revenue and total tax revenue

− 2 Equation about relationship between growth of total fiscal revenue and growth of total tax revenue

(2) − 1 Equation about relationship between total tax revenue and GDP

- 2 Equation about relationship between growth of total tax revenue and GDP growth

(3) - 1 Equation about relationship between revenue from value-added tax and growth of total industrial added values

- 2 Equation about relationship between revenue from value-added tax and ultimate consumption

(4) Equation about relationship between revenue from business tax, value added by the sector of real estate among value added by the tertiary industry, value added by the sector of construction and total investment in fixed assets in the secondary industry

(5) Equation about relationship between revenue from customs duties, total tax revenue and exchange rate

4.3.1.2 Revenue growth model is designed with 4 equations

(1) Equation for analyzing contributions by growth rates of central government revenue and local governments revenue to growth rate of total fiscal revenue

(2) Equation about relationship between growth rate of total tax revenue and GDP growth rate

(3) Equation about relationship between growth rate of fiscal revenue and that of the sum of value added of the secondary and tertiary industries

(4) Equation about relationship between growth rates of total fiscal revenue, revenue from business tax and revenue from value-added tax

4.3.2 Econometric models for fiscal expenditures

Econometric models of fiscal expenditures include total expenditure model and expenditure growth model

4.3.2.1 Total expenditure model is designed with 6 equations

(1) Equation about relationship between total fiscal expenditure, total fiscal revenue and GDP

(2) Equation about relationship between spending on general public services and fiscal revenue

(3) Equation about spending on education

(4) Equation about relationship between spending on science and technology, and fiscal revenue

(5) Equation about relationship between spending on social security and

employment and fiscal revenue

(6) Equation about spending on environment protection

4.3.2.2 Expenditure growth model is designed with 2 equations

(1) Equation for analyzing contributions by growth rates of central expenditures and local expenditures to growth rate of total fiscal expenditures

(2) Equation for analyzing contributions by growth rates of spending on general public services, spending on education, spending on social security and employment, and spending on environment protection to growth rate of total fiscal expenditures

4.3.3 The model for economic growth and its components is designed with 5 equations

(1) Equation about relationship between GDP growth in the broad sense and growths of total consumption, total investment in fixed assets, balance of exports and imports

(2) Equation for analyzing contributions by log growth rate of fiscal expenditure in final accounts to GDP growth rate

(3) Equation for analyzing contributions by growth rates of values added by the primary industry, the secondary industry and the tertiary industry to GDP growth rate

(4) Equation for analyzing contributions by growth rates of total industrial output values and values added by the sector of construction to growth rate of values added by the secondary industry

4.4 Running results of econometric models for China's public finance and taxation

4.4.1 Running results of econometric models for fiscal revenue

4.4.1.1 Running results of total revenue model

4.4.1.1.1 Equation about relationship between total fiscal revenue and total tax revenue

(1) When the sample period is from 1979 to 2011, first implement a stationarity and unit root test of total fiscal revenue ($\ln rev_t = \ln(rev_t)$) and total tax revenue ($\ln tax_t = \ln(tax_t)$), with the ADF statistics respectively of 4.376 and 0.282. The ADF statistics of differentiated total positive fiscal rev-

enue ($\Delta \ln rev_t = \ln rev_t - \ln rev_{t-1}$) and total tax revenue ($\Delta \ln tax_t = \ln tax_t - \ln tax_{t-1}$) are -2.865 and -5.419 respectively, both passing the stationarity test[1]. Therefore, it can be known that total fiscal revenue and total tax revenue are both integrated time series of order one. To examine whether both of them have the same variation, that is, whether they are co-integrated, it is required to implement a co-integration test. Here, Engle and Granger co-integration test (1987)[2] is adopted and the statistical amount is -1.753, passing the test at the level of 1% [3], indicating that they are co-integrated. Then, estimate the co-integration equation between both of them. Here, the Engle and Granger (1987) two-step method, namely, the error correction method, is adopted to estimate the cointegration.

① Equation about relationship between total fiscal revenue ($\ln rev_t = \ln (rev_t)$) and total tax revenue ($\ln tax_t = \ln(tax_t)$) :

The co-integration estimation formula is

$$\ln rev_t = -0.1627 + 1.1576 \ln tax_t$$
$$(0.37) \qquad (16.45)$$

This indicates that estimated as per the annual data, the elasticity of total fiscal revenue to total tax revenue in the long run is 1.1576. That is to say, for every 1% growth of total tax revenue, total fiscal revenue shall increase by around an average of 1.1576%.

② Equation about relationship between growth of total fiscal revenue ($\Delta \ln rev_t$) and delayed growth of total tax revenue ($\Delta \ln tax_{t-1}$) :

Next, estimate the error correction model. Here, the Engle and Granger (1987) two-step method, namely, the error correction method, is adopted. The coefficient of error correction item reflects the adjustment of short-term deviation from long-term equilibrium path. The coefficient is -0.0105, indi-

---

① The critical value of ADF statistic is -3.702 at 1% significant level, -2.980 at 5% significant level, and -2.622 at 10% significant level. Critical values of unit root tests for the following variables are the same (Makinon, 2010).

② Engle, R. F. and Granger, C. W. J. 1987. "Co-integration and Error Correction: Representation, Estimation and Testing"Econometrica, Vol. 55, pp. 251-76

③ The critical value of ADF statistic of Engle and Granger (1987) co-integration test is -3.654 at 1% significant level, -2.957 at 5% significant level and -2.618 at 10% significant level. Critical values of the statistics of the following co-integration tests are the same.

cating that when short-term fluctuation deviates from long-term equilibrium, it shall be dragged back from the position of disequilibrium to one of equilibrium by a power of -0.0105, and the average adjustment each year is about 1% compared with its previous year.

The error correction equation is:

$$\Delta\ln rev_t = 0.0597 - 0.0105 ecm_{t-1} - 0.2035\Delta\ln tax_{t-1} + 0.8257\Delta\ln rev_{t-1}$$
$$(0.0213) \quad (0.0249) \quad\quad (0.0833) \quad\quad\quad (0.2049)$$

4.4.1.1.2 Equation about relationship between total tax revenue and GDP

(1) When the sample period is from 1979 to 2011, first implement a stationarity and unit root test of GDP ($\ln gdp_t = \ln(gdp_t)$) with the ADF statistic of -0.159. Unit root ADF statistic of differentiated GDP ($\Delta\ln gdp_t = \ln gdp_{it} - \ln gdp_{it-1}$) is -3.902, which shows that GDP ($\ln gdp_t = \ln(gdp_{it})$) is an integrated variable of order one. It can be known from tests in the above that total tax revenue ($\ln tax_t$) is also an integrated variable of order one. Next, examine whether both of them are co-integrated. First, implement the Engle and Granger co-integration test (1987) with the statistic of -1.428, indicating that they are significantly co-integrated (at the level of 1%).

① Equation about relationship between total tax revenue ($\ln tax_t$) and GDP ($\ln gdp_t = \ln(gdp_{it})$):

$$\ln tax_t = -1.78087 + 1.0411\ln gdp_t$$
$$(-1.32) \quad\quad (14.63)$$

Running result of the model: apart from operation by its own inertia rules, total tax revenue is significantly dependent on national economic growth. Estimated by annual data, long-term elasticity of total tax revenue to GDP is about 1.0411, indicating that for every 1% of GDP growth, total tax revenue shall increase by 1.0537% on average. This explains that growth of total tax revenue fails to keep pace with GDP growth. Growth of tax burdens on the economy is slightly faster than that of national economy. For instance, the higher enterprise profitability is, the greater the growth of revenue from income tax, and the growth of net profits shall be correspondingly reduced. Similarly, growth of revenue from individual income tax shall reduce growth of labor incomes. If this continues for a long period, it shall be ill to sustainable economic growth. That means China's tax regime needs to be further adjusted to create a better space for economies to develop.

② Equation about relationship between growth of total tax revenue ($\Delta \ln tax_t$) and delayed GDP growth ($\Delta \ln gdp_{t-1}$):

$$\Delta \ln tax_t = 0.0328 + 0.3785 \Delta \ln gdp_{t-1} + 0.0059 \Delta \ln tax_{t-1} + 0.1289 ecm_{t-1}$$
$$(0.0903) \quad (0.4148) \qquad\quad (0.2053) \qquad\qquad (0.1203)$$

The result of the empirical analysis through the error correction model is: The coefficient of error correction item ecm_{t-1} reflects the adjustment of short-term deviation from long-term equilibrium path. The coefficient is 0.1289, indicating that when short-term fluctuation deviates from long-term equilibrium, it shall be dragged back from the position of disequilibrium to one of equilibrium by a power of 0.1289, and the average adjustment each year is about 12% compared with its previous year.

4.4.1.1.3 Equation about relationship between revenue from value-added tax and growth of total industrial added values

(1) When the sample period is from 1986 to 2011, first implement a stationarity and unit root test of revenue from value-added tax ($\ln vat_t = \ln (vat_t)$) and industrial added values ($\ln ivi_t = \ln (incresed\ value\ of\ industry_t)$) with the ADF statistics of -1.719 and -1.367 respectively. ADF statistics of differentiated revenue from value-added tax ($\Delta \ln vat_t = \ln vat_t - \ln vat_{t-1}$) and industrial added values ($\Delta \ln ivi_t = \ln ivi_t - \ln ivi_{t-1}$) are -4.047 and -5.583, both passing the stationarity test. It can be known that revenue from value-added tax and total industrial added values are both integrated variables of order one. To examine whether both of them change in the same way, that is, whether they are co-integrated, it is required to conduct the co-integration test. Here, the Engle and Granger co-integration test (1987) is implemented with the statistic of -2.850, passing the test at 5% significant level. That indicates that they are co-integrated.

① Equation about relationship between revenue from value-added tax ($\ln vat_t = \ln (vat_t)$) and growth of industrial added values ($\ln ivi_t = \ln (incresed\ value\ of\ industry_t)$):

$$\ln vat_t = 1.1355 + 0.2262 \ln ivi_t$$
$$(2.31) \quad (3.54)$$

Running result of the model: dependence of revenue from value-added tax on industrial added values is 0.2262. During the modeling, we find that regression coefficients of value-added tax and growth of industrial added values are not very significant, with certain dis-coordination. The reasons are multiple, including the taxation system, collection and management level, changes to the economic structure, economic and taxation differences in calculation and statistics. Of course, as the sample period of China's value-added tax is short in itself, tax reform is in progress, running results of this equation may be to some degree distorted.

(2) With the gradual implementation of China's tax reform, value-added tax has transformed from a production type to a consumption type. To this end, we build the model ② to study long-term impacts of ultimate consumption on revenue from value-added tax.

When the sample period is from 1985 to 2011, first implement a stationarity and unit root test of ultimate consumption ($\ln fvc_t$ = $\ln$(*final value of consumption*$_t$)) with the ADF statistic of -0.321. ADF statistic of differentiated ultimate consumption ($\ln fvc_t = \ln fvc_t - \ln fvc_{t-1}$) are -4.047 and -4.369. It can be known that ultimate consumption $\ln fvc_t$ is an integrated time series of order one. From the above, we know that value-added tax $\ln vat_t$ is also an integrated time series of order one. To examine whether both of them change in the same way, that is, whether they are co-integrated, it is required to conduct the co-integration test. Here, the Engle and Granger co-integration test (1987) is implemented with the statistic of -1.632, passing the test at 1% significant level. That indicates that they are co-integrated.

② Equation about relationship between revenue from value-added tax ($\ln vat_t$) and ultimate consumption ($\ln fvc_t$):

$$\ln vat_t = -4.3180 + 1.2677 \ln fvc_t$$
$$(2.12) \qquad (4.20)$$

Based on long-term co-integration, the growth of revenue from value-added tax is several percentage points higher than that of ultimate consumption; that is, for every 1% of growth in ultimate consumption, revenue from value-added tax shall increase by 1.2677%.

4.4.1.1.4 Equation about relationship between revenue from business tax, values added by the sector of real estate among values added by the tertiary industry, values added by the sector of construction and total investment on fixed assets in the secondary industry

When the sample period is from 1985 to 2011, first implement a stationarity and unit root test of revenue from business tax ($\ln tut_t = \ln(turnover\ taxation_t)$) and values added by the sector of real estate ($\ln var_t = \ln(value\ added\ of\ real\ estate_t)$) in values added of the tertiary industry, values added by the sector of construction ($\ln vaa_t = \ln(value\ added\ of\ architecture_t)$) and total investment on fixed assets in the secondary industry ($\ln ifc_t = \ln(investment\ of\ fixxed\ capital_t)$). Corresponding ADF statistics are 18.147, -1.932, -1.227 and 0.227 respectively. ADF statistics of relative variables differentiated are -6.986, -4.199, -4.419 and -4.727. Therefore, it can be known that they are all integrated time series of order one. To examine whether both of them change in the same way, that is, whether they are co-integrated, it is required to conduct the co-integration test. Here, we continue to use the Engle and Granger co-integration test (1987) with the statistic of -2.638, which passes the test at 1% significant level, indicating that they are co-integrated.

Equation about relationship between revenue from business tax ($\ln tut_t$), values added by the sector of real estate among values added by the tertiary industry ($\ln var_t$), values added by the sector of construction ($\ln vaa_t$) and total investment in fixed assets ($\ln ifc_t$) in the secondary industry:

$$\ln tut_t = -0.6872 + 0.1720\ln var_t - 0.0642\ln vaa_t + 0.6734\ln ifc_t$$
$$(2.15) \quad (1.13) \quad (-7.23) \quad (3.25)$$

Running result of the model: revenue from business tax in the current year significantly depends on values added by the sector of real estate, the sector of construction and total investment in fixed assets. The elasticity of revenue from business tax to values added by the sector of real estate is 0.1720, that is, for every 1% of values added by the sector of real estate, business tax shall grow by 0.1720%, indicating that the sector of real estate in the tertiary industry is important to promote revenue from business tax. The elasticity of total investment in fixed assets to business incomes is 0.6734, indicating that for every 1% of growth in total investment in fixed assets, revenue from business tax shall rose up by 0.6734%, a growth higher than the result brought up by values added by the sector of real estate in the tertiary industry. Total investment in fixed assets has certain impacts on revenue from business tax, because it basically represents the investment level of the entire society and naturally has positive relations with development of the entire economy.

4.4.1.1.5 Equation about relationship between revenue from customs duties, total tax revenue and exchange rate

When the sample period is from 1986 to 2011, first it is required to implement a stationarity and unit root test of revenue from customs duties ($\ln dut_t$ = $\ln(duty\ taxation_t)$), total tax revenue ($\ln tax_t$) and exchange rate ($\ln rfe_t$ = $\ln(rate\ of\ foreign\ exchange)$). Level values of the ADF statistics are 0.440, 2.843 and -2.454 respectively. ADF statistics of differentiated values are -5.375, -4.655 and -4.075 respectively, indicating the three variables are all integrate processes of order one. To examine whether the three variables change in the same way, that is, whether they are co-integrated, it is required to conduct the co-integration test. Here, we continue to use the Engle and Granger co-integration test (1987) with the statistic of -3.112, passing the test at 1% significant level. That indicates that they are co-integrated.

Equation about relationship between revenue from customs duties ($\ln dut_t$), total tax revenue ($\ln tax_t$) and exchange rate ($\ln rfe_t$):

$$\ln dut_t = -5.871 + 0.9695 \ln tax_t + 0.6120 \ln rfe_t$$
$$(-1.24)\quad (10.44)\qquad (1.85)$$

Running result of the model: the coefficient of customs duties to tax revenue is positive, indicating that revenue from customs duties changes in the same direction with tax revenue and shall grow up by 0.9695% for every 1% of growth in tax revenue. The elasticity of revenue from customs duties to exchange rate is 0.6120, meaning that Renminbi depreciation can promote the growth of revenue from customs duties. Revenue from customs duties significantly depends on total tax revenue and exchange rate.

4.4.1.2 Running results of revenue growth model

(1) Equation for analyzing contributions by growth rates of central government revenue and local governments revenue to growth rate of total fiscal

revenue

When the sample period is from 1980 to 2011, it is required to implement a unit root test of growth rates of total fiscal revenue ($rtr_t = rate\ of\ total\ revenue\ increased$), central revenue ($rcr_t = rate\ of\ central\ revenue\ increased$) and local revenue ($rlr_t = rate\ of\ local\ revenue\ increased$). Corresponding ADF statistics are -4.057, -5.321 and -4.324 respectively, indicating that the three variables are stable. Therefore, it is feasible to implement the ordinary least-squares regression.

① Equation for analyzing contributions by growth rates of central government revenue ($rcr_t = rate\ of\ central\ revenue\ increased$) and local governments revenue ($rlr_t = rate\ of\ local\ revenue\ increased$) to growth rate of total fiscal revenue ($rtr_t = rate\ of\ total\ revenue\ increased$) [①]:

$$rtr_t = 16.0454 + 0.3345 rcr_t + 0.6440 rlr_t - 11.0422 d94 - 11.2623 d95$$
$$\quad (4.8421)\ (0.0289)\quad (0.0270)\quad (24.5360)\quad (24.4753)$$
$$\quad -11.3175 d05$$
$$\quad (24.4710)$$
$$R^2 = 0.9891 \quad SSE = 0.0023 \quad DW = 2.4035$$

Running result of the model: dependence of the growth rate of total fiscal revenue on that of central revenue is 0.6440, which indicates that the growth rate of total fiscal revenue significantly depends on growth rates of central and local revenue.

(2) Equation about relationship between growth rate of total tax revenue and GDP growth rate

When the sample period is from 1986 to 2011, it is known from the above that growth of total tax revenue is stable. Next, it is required to implement a stationarity and unit root test of GDP growth rate with the ADF statistic of -4.578. It can be known that GDP growth rate is also a stable process. Therefore, it is feasible to implement the ordinary least-squares regression.

② Equation about relationship between growth rate of total tax revenue (rtr_t) and GDP growth rate ($rgdp_t = rate\ of\ GDP\ increased$):

---

① Here, d94, d95 and d05 stands for virtual time variables of 1994, 1995 and 2005.

$$rtr_t = 4.7742 + 0.9167rgdp_t$$
$$(5.8146) \quad (0.6131)$$
$$R^2 = 0.9105 \quad SSE = 0.1335 \quad DW = 2.2542$$

Running result of the model: dependence of the growth rate of total tax revenue on GDP growth rate is 0.9167, up by 0.1094 compared with the previous year, indicating that the growth rate of total tax revenue significantly depends on GDP growth rate. During the sample period, the average growth rate of total tax revenue is 20.11%, 4.39 percentage points higher that the average GDP growth rate of 15.72%. Notably, tax revenue that grows up faster than national revenue shall produce negative impacts on the economy. To maintain long-term steady and balanced economic development, it is a must to advance tax reform, and at the same time, pay attention to implement structural tax reduction to reduce tax burden by means of tax reduction, rebate and exemption, promote enterprise investment and resident consumption, implement a positive fiscal policy and boost the steady and healthy development of the national economy so as to have favorable impacts on tax revenue.

(3) Equation about relationship between growth rate of total fiscal revenue and that of the sum of value added of the secondary and tertiary industries

When the sample period is from 1980 to 2011, it is required to implement unit root tests of growth rate of total fiscal revenue (rtr_t) and growth rates of the sum of values added by the secondary and tertiary industries (rfs_t = *rate of increased value added of first and second industry*). The ADF statistics are -3.958 and -4.052 respectively, indicating that both are stable processes. Therefore, it is feasible to implement the ordinary least-squares regression.

③ Equation about relationship between growth rate of total fiscal revenue (rtr_t) and that of the sum of value added of the secondary and tertiary industries (rfs_t):

$$rtr_t = 0.0445 + 0.4503rfs_t$$
$$(2.6701) \quad (2.2525)$$
$$R^2 = 0.5135 \quad SSE = 0.1658 \quad DW = 2.5542$$

Running result of the model: dependence of the growth rate of the sum of values added by the secondary and the tertiary industries on the growth rate of total fiscal revenue is 0.4503, indicating that values added by the secondary and the tertiary industries have made significant contributions to the growth of total fiscal revenue.

(4) Equation about relationship between growth rates of total fiscal revenue, revenue from business tax and revenue from value-added tax

When the sample period is from 1985 to 2011, it is required to implement ADF stationarity test of growth rate of total fiscal revenue (rtr_t), growth rates of revenue from business tax ($rtut_t$) and revenue from value-added tax ($rvat_t$). The ADF statistics are -4.354, -3.995 and -5.032 respectively, indicating that they are stable. Therefore, it is feasible to implement the ordinary least-squares regression.

④ Equation about relationship between growth rates of total fiscal revenue (rtr_t), revenue from business tax ($rtut_t$) and revenue from value-added tax ($rvat_t$):

$$rtr_t = 0.1573 + 0.0310 rtut_t + 0.0274 rvat_t$$
$$(5.1011) \quad (2.7321) \quad (2.0504)$$
$$R^2 = 0.8246 \quad SSE = 0.1243 \quad DW = 2.0011$$

Running result of the model: dependence of the growth rate of revenue from business tax on the growth rate of total fiscal revenue is 0.0310, while dependence of the growth rate of revenue from value-added tax on the growth rate of total fiscal revenue is 0.0274.

4.4.2 Running results of econometric models for fiscal expenditures

Analysis on results of econometric models for fiscal expenditures is divided into 3 parts: analysis of total expenditures, analysis of expenditure growth and that of economic growth.

4.4.2.1 Running results of total expenditure model

(1) Equation about relationship between total fiscal expenditure, total fiscal revenue and GDP

Apart from operation in line with its own inertia rules, total fiscal expenditure significantly depends on total fiscal revenue and GDP.

When the sample period is from 1979 to 2011, first it is required to implement a stationarity and unit root test of growth of total fiscal expenditure in the broad sense ($lnexp_t = ln(total\ fscal\ exp\ enditure)$). The ADF statistic is 1.040. ADF statistic of differentiated values is -3.079, indicating that it is n integrate process at the 5% level. Combined with results of unit root tests in the above, it can be known that total fiscal expenditure ($\ln exp_t$), total fiscal revenue ($\ln rev_t$) and GDP ($\ln gdp_t$) are all integrated processes of order one. To examine whether both of them change in the same way, that is, whether they are co-integrated, it is required to conduct the co-integration test. Here, we continue to use the Engle and Granger co-integration test (1987) with the statistic of -2.548, passing the test at 1% significant level. That indicates that they are co-integrated.

① Equation about relationship between total fiscal expenditure ($\ln exp_t$), total fiscal revenue ($\ln rev_t$) and GDP ($\ln gdp_t$):

$$\ln exp_t = -0.1775 + 0.8821 \ln rev_t + 0.1209 \ln gdp_t$$
$$(1.37) \quad (27.80) \quad (3.90)$$

Running result of the model: the elasticity of total fiscal expenditure is 0.9372 to total fiscal revenue and 0.1209 to GDP, indicating that with the economic growth, fiscal expenditure is also growing. Demand of economic growth for fiscal expenditure remains positive. Excluding operation in line with its own inertia rules, the elasticity of total fiscal expenditure to fiscal revenue is 0.8821, indiciating that the growth of fiscal revenue shall lead to the growth of fiscal expenditure and that fiscal expenditure significantly depends on total fiscal revenue and GDP.

(2) Equation about relationship between spending on general public services and fiscal revenue

When the sample period is from January 2007 to December 2012, it is required to implement stationarity and unit root test of spending on general public services ($\lg pe_t = general\ public\ service\ exp\ enditure$) and fiscl revenue ($lrev_t = \ln(rev_t)$). The ADF statistics are -5.641 and -3.931 respectively, indicating that they are stable. Therefore, it is feasible to estimate with the ordinary least-squares regression.

② Equation about relationship between spending on general public services ($\lg pe_t = \ln(general\ public\ service\ exp\ enditure_t)$) and fiscal revenue ($lrev_t = \ln(rev_t)$):

$$\lg pe_t = 3.9233 + 0.3024 lrev_t$$
$$(4.26) \quad (2.87)$$
$$R^2 = 0.7963 \quad SSE = 4.4608 \quad DW = 2.5622$$

Running result of the model shows that for every 1% of growth in fiscal revenue, spending on general public services shall grow up by 0.3024%. As spending on general public services accounts for a small proportion in total fiscal expenditure, this indicates that spending on general public services is not enough, so the government should further increase the proportion of spending on general public services.

(3) Equation about spending on education

Spending on education significantly depends on that of the previous period. When the sample period is from January 2007 to December 2012, ADF statistic of the level value of spending on education ($lfee_t = \ln(fiscal$ exp $enditure\ of\ educaation_t)$) is -5.092, indicating that it is stable. Fiscal revenue ($lrev_t$) is also stable, as shown in the above. Therefore, it is feasible to estimate with the ordinary least-squares regression.

③ Equation about spending on education ($lfee_t$):

$$lfee_t = 6.7092 + 0.5228 lfee_{t-1}$$
$$(2.23) \quad (2.78)$$
$$R^2 = 0.9963 \quad SSE = 5235.56 \quad DW = 2.5622$$

Running result of the model: dependence of spending on education on its previous period is 0.5228, indicating that spending on education has the intertia to increase over the previous period, that is, if spending on education increased in the previous period, it shall have more increases in next period. During the modeling, we find that dependence of spending on education on fiscal revenue is not obvious and the growth rate of spending on education is substantially lower than that of fiscal reveneu and the economy. The country's input on education is not enough. So it is necessary to increase spending on education.

(4) Equation about relationship between spending on science and technology, and fiscal revenue

When the sample period is from January 2007 to December 2012, the stationarity test is passed. ADF statistic of spending on science and technology ($lfes_t = \ln(fiscal$ exp $enditure\ of\ science_t)$) is -4.109, indicating that it is stable. Fiscal revenue ($lrev_t$) is also stable as shown in the above. Therefore, it is feasible to estimate with the ordinary least-squares regression.

④ Equation about relationship between spending on science and technology ($lfes_t = \ln(fiscal\ exp\ enditure\ of\ science_t)$) and fiscal revenue ($lrev_t$):

$$lfes_t = -5.0345 + 1.1602lrev_t$$
$$(-2.34)\quad(4.72)$$
$$R^2 = 0.6827\quad SSE = 1.6531\quad DW = 2.7613$$

Estimated result of the model shows that the elasticity of spending on science and technology is 1.1602. That is, for every 1% of growth in fiscal revenue, spending on science and technology shall grow up by 1.1602%.

(5) Equation about relationship between spending on social security and employment and fiscal revenue

When the sample period is from January 2007 to December 2012, the stationarity test is passed. ADF statistics of spending on social security and employment ($lfese_t = \ln(fiscal\ exp\ enditure\ of\ social\ security\ and\ employment_t)$) and fiscal revenue ($lrev_t$) are -3.797 and -3.755 respectively, indicating that they are stable. Therefore, it is feasible to estimate with the ordinary least-squares regression.

⑤ Error correction equation about relationship between spending on social security and employment ($lfese_t$) and fiscal revenue ($lrev_t$):

$$lfese_t = -0.2259 + 0.7599lrev_t$$
$$(-0.21)\quad(6.25)$$
$$R^2 = 0.7827\quad SSE = 1.3068\quad DW = 2.5623$$

Running result of the model shows that the elasticity of spending on social security and employment is 0.7599. That is, for every 1% of growth in fiscal revenue, spending on social security and employment shall grow up by 0.7599%. During the national economic growth, investment in people's livelihood should be gradually increased. At present, its proportion is very small. So we need to further increase spending on social security and employment.

(6) Equation about spending on environment protection

When the sample period is from January 2007 to December 2012, through the stationarity test, ADF statistic of spending on envrionment protection ($lfeep_t = \ln(fiscal\ exp\ enditure\ of\ environment\ protection_t)$) is -3.095, indicating that it is stable. Fiscal revenue ($lrev_t$) is also stable, as shown in the above. Therefore, it is feasible to estimate with the ordinary least-squares regression.

⑥ Error correction equation about relationship between spending on environment protection ($lfeep_t$) and fiscal revenue ($lrev_t$) :

$$lfeep_t = -6.0439 + 0.2134 lrev_t$$
$$(-2.55) \quad (4.48)$$
$$R^2 = 0.8156 \quad SSE = 2.1068 \quad DW = 2.4521$$

Running result of the above model shows that the elasticity of spending on environment protection is 0.2134. That is, for every 1% of growth in fiscal revenue, spending on environment protection shall grow up by 0.2134%. This indicates that spending on environment protection is too low, so the government should increase more spending on environment protection in the future.

4.4.2.2 Running results of expenditure growth model

(1) Equation for analyzing contributions by growth rates of central government expenditures and local governments expenditures to growth rate of total fiscal expenditures

When the sample period is from 1979 to 2011, the unit root test is passed. ADF statistics of growth rates of central expenditure (rce_t = rate of increased centural fiscal expenditure), local expenditure (rle_t = rate of increased local fiscal expenditure) and total fiscal expenditure (rte_t = rate of increased total fiscal expenditure) are -3.967, -4.684 and -4.012 respectively, indicating that they are all stable. Therefore, it is feasible to estimate with the ordinary least-squares regression.

① Equation for analyzing contributions by growth rates of central expenditures (rce_t) and local expenditures (rle_t) to growth rate of total fiscal expenditures (rte_t) :

$$rte_t = 3.1455 + 0.5357 rle_t + 0.4623 rce_t$$
$$(1.0486) \quad (0.0131) \quad (0.0367)$$
$$R^2 = 0.9827 \quad SSE = 0.0109 \quad DW = 2.3077$$

Running result of the model: dependence of the growth rate of total fiscal expenditure on growth rates of central and local expenditures are 0.4623 and 0.5357 respectively. By further calculating their average growth rates in 1979 ~ 2011, it can be known that the average growth rate of local expenditures was 16.55%, higher than that of central expenditure at 12.31%, indicating that the growth rate of total fiscal expenditure significantly depends on growth rates of central and local expenditures.

(2) Equation for analyzing contributions by growth rates of spending on

general public services, spending on education, spending on social security and employment, and spending on environment protection to growth rate of total fiscal expenditures

When the sample period is from January 2007 to December 2012, growth rates of spending on general public services, spending on education, spending on science and technology, spending on social security and employment, spending on environment protection and fiscal expenditure pass the stationarity test. Their ADF statistics are -3.948, -4.021, -3.932, -4.351 and -3.875 respectively.

② Regression equation between growth rate of total fiscal expenditures (rte_t) and growth rates of spending on general public services ($rgpe_t$), spending on education ($rfee_t$), spending on social security and employment ($rfese_t$) and spending on environment protection ($rfeep_t$) (here the values represent the percentages):

$$rte_t = 7.0152 + 0.1928rgpe_t + 0.1219rfee_t + 0.4029rfese_t + 0.1847rfeep_t$$
$$(1.28) \quad (1.00) \qquad (3.76) \qquad (1.81) \qquad (1.68)$$
$$R^2 = 0.8502 \quad SSE = 10672 \quad DW = 2.4522$$

The regression result shows that contribution made by the growth rate of spending on education to the growth rate of total fiscal expenditure is 0.1219, that by the growth rate of spending on social security 0.4029 and that by the growth rate of spending on environment protection 0.1847, but that by the growth rate of spending on general public services is not significant.

4.4.2.3 Running results of the model for economic growth and its components

(1) Equation about relationship between GDP growth in the broad sense and growths of total consumption, total investment in fixed assets, balance of exports and imports

When the sample period is from 1981 to 2011, the stationarity test is passed. It can be known that GDP growth in the broad sense, growths of total consumption, total investment in fixed assets and balance of exports and imports are all integrated time series of order one. ADF statistics of their level values are -2.234, -2.124 and -1.321 respectively, while that of their differentiated values are -3.984, -4.042 and -4.113 respectively, indicating that these variables are integrated processes of order one. The statistic of the Engle and Granger co-integration test (1987) is −4.357, meaning that these variables are co-integrated. Running result of the error correction equation:

① Error correction equation about relationship between GDP growth in the broad sense (Δgdp_t) and growths of total consumption (Δtc_t), total investment in fixed assets (Δifc_t), balance of exports and imports (Δexm_t):

$$\Delta gdp_t = -55.9917 - 3.1353 ecm_{t-1} + 2.5211 \Delta gdp_{t-1} - 4.5099 \Delta tc_{t-1}$$
$$(-0.06) \quad (-8.89) \quad (7.72) \quad (-4.78)$$
$$+ 2.6635 \Delta ifc_{t-1} + 0.0371 \Delta exm_{t-1}$$
$$(8.34) \quad (0.06)$$

Based on the error correction model, the coefficient of error correction item reflects the adjustment of short-term deviation from long-term equilibrium path. The coefficient is −3.1353, indicating that when short-term fluctuation deviates from long-term equilibrium, it shall be dragged back from the position of disequilibrium to one of equilibrium by a power of 3.1353.

(2) Equation for analyzing contributions by delayed growth rate of fiscal expenditure in final accounts to GDP growth rate

When the sample period is from 1981 to 2011, through the stationarity test, ADF statistics of GDP growth rate ($rgdp_t$) and delayed growth rate of fiscal expenditure in final accounts (rte_{t-1}) are −3.969 and −4.681, both stable processes.

② Regression equation between GDP growth rate ($rgdp_t$) and delayed growth rate of fiscal expenditure in final accounts (rte_{t-1}):

$$rgdp_t = 0.0711 + 0.5947 rte_{t-1}$$
$$(2.77) \quad (4.01)$$
$$R^2 = 0.8734 \quad SSE = 0.8045 \quad DW = 1.2243$$

It can be known from analysis by means of the general linear regression that contribution by the lag in the growth rate of fiscal expenditure in final accounts to GDP growth rate is 59.47%.

(3) Equation for analyzing contributions by growth rates of value added by the primary industry, the secondary industry and the tertiary industry to GDP growth rate

When the sample period is from 1978 to 2011, ADF statistics of growth rates of values added by the primary industry (rfi_t), the secondary industry

(rsi_t) and the tertiary industry (rti_t) to GDP growth rate ($rgdp_t$) are −3.578, −4.264, −4.132 and −4.056 respectively, passing the stationarity test.

③ Equation for analyzing contributions by growth rates of values added by the primary industry (rfi_t), the secondary industry (rsi_t) and the tertiary industry (rti_t) to GDP growth rate ($rgdp_t$):

$$rgdp_t = 0.0249 + 0.2435rfi_t + 0.5627rsi_t + 0.2376rti_t$$
$$(4.7302)(0.0243) \quad (0.0165) \quad (0.0143)$$
$$R^2 = 0.9739 \quad SSE = 0.0149 \quad DW = 2.3451$$

Running result of the model: dependence of GDP growth rate on growth rates of values added by the primary industry, the secondary industry and the tertiary industry are 0.2435, 0.5711 and 0.2499 respectively, indicating that GDP growth rate significantly depends on growth rates of values added by the primary industry, the secondary industry and the tertiary industry

(4) Equation for analyzing contributions by growth rates of total industrial output values and values added by the sector of construction to growth rate of values added by the secondary industry

When the sample period is from 1978 to 2011, ADF statistics of growth rates of total industrial output values ($ravi_t$ rll1) and values added by the sector of construction ($rava_t$ rll14) are −3.785 and −4.317 respectively, passing the stationarity test.

④ Equation for analyzing contributions by growth rates of total industrial output values ($ravi_t$ rll1) and values added by the sector of construction ($rava_t$ rll14) to the growth rate of values added by the secondary industry (rsi_t rll66):

$$rsi_t = 6.1033 + 0.8726ravi_t + 0.1723rava_t$$
$$(2.2540)(0.0168) \quad (0.0871)$$
$$R^2 = 0.9825 \quad SSE = 1.2754 \quad DW = 2.5744$$

Running result of the model: dependence of the growth rate of values added by the secondary industry on growth rates of total industrial output values and values added by the sector of construction are 0.8726 and 0.1723 respectively, indicating that the growth rate of values added by the secondary industry significantly depends on growth rates of total industrial output values and values added by the sector of construction.

4.4.3 Forecasts for major fiscal and macroeconomic indicators

Combined with our understanding and command of China's fiscal and e-conomic operation rules and mechanisms, we have made short-term forecasts for China's major fiscal and macroeconomic indicators, the main method being to forecast 3 steps forward by using the fcast command in Stata on the basis of estimated results of econometric models. (See in Table 4.2).

Table 4.2 Forecasts for Major Fiscal and Macroeconomic Indicators

Economic variables	2011	2012	2013
Total fiscal revenue	10 387.48 310*	11 951.60 699	13 751.03 713
Total tax revenue	89 738.39 732*	99 950.93 665	100 552.406 756
Total fiscal expenditures	109 247.798 902*	127 580.033 792	145 523.319 235
GDP	472 881.337 022*	531 635.199 869	581 437.690 193
Revenue from value-added tax	24 266.63 693*	28 714.56 519	33 476.72 351
Central government revenue	42 488.47 712*	51 798.73 064	63 063.42 228
Local governments revenue	40 613.04 727*	45 594.56 944	51 244.59 629
Central government expenditures	15 989.73 279*	17 952.59 951	20 140.93 517
Local government expenditure	73 884.43 610*	84 093.58 766	97 248.60 023
Added values of the primary industry	47 712.50 433*	52 377.23 291*	57 872.76 340
Added values of the secondary industry	220 591.187 681*	235 319.475 145*	268 817.393 035
Added values of the tertiary industry	203 260.173 087*	231 626.391 842*	269 863.821 206
Industrial added values	188 571.760 867*	199 860.581 457*	228 725.529 543
Values added by the sector of construction	32 019.86 714*	35 459.06 973*	41 285.25 327
Total investment in fixed assets	311 485.124 379*	369 604.863 795	442 664.826 744
Ultimate consumption	183 918.673 734*	212 445.237 965	245 247.279 031
Consumer price index	105.4%*	105.8%	106.2%

Notes: Values marked with * are taken from China Statistical Yearbook 2012 and CEInet database.

Estimated results in Table 4. 2 shows that without change to the data, major variables, such as total fiscal revenue, total tax revenue, total fiscal expenditures, GDP, revenue from value-added tax, central revenue, local revenue, central expenditure and local expenditure, shall continue to increase in 2012 and 2013. Among them, total tax revenue, total fiscal expenditure, GDP and revenue from value-added tax shall slow down in growth, and total fiscal revenue and central revenue shall roughly remain the same growth in 2012 and 2013, while the growth of local expenditure shall be on the rise in 2013.

References:

1. Engle, R. F. and Granger, C. W. J. 1987. "Co-integration and Error Correction: Representation, Estimation and Testing", Econometrica, Vol. 55, pp. 251-76

2. MacKinnon, James G. , 2010. "Critical Values for Cointegration Tests. " Queen's Economics Department Working Paper No. 1227.

3. Hu Yijian, 2008: A Textbook of Taxation, Gezhi Press.

4. Jiang Hong, Zhu Ping, 2011: Public Economics, 2nd ed. , Shanghai University of Finance and Economics Press.